Media & Mental Health

Health Communication

Gary L. Kreps, Series Editor

Vol. 17

The Health Communication series is part of
the Peter Lang Media and Communication list.
Every volume is peer reviewed and meets
the highest quality standards for content and production.

PETER LANG
New York • Berlin • Brussels • Lausanne • Oxford

Scott Parrott

Media & Mental Health

Using Mass Media to Reduce the Stigma of Mental Illness

PETER LANG
New York • Berlin • Brussels • Lausanne • Oxford

Library of Congress Cataloging-in-Publication Control Number: 2022044445

Bibliographic information published by **Die Deutsche Nationalbibliothek**.
Die Deutsche Nationalbibliothek lists this publication in the "Deutsche Nationalbibliografie"; detailed bibliographic data are available on the Internet at http://dnb.d-nb.de/.

ISSN 2153-1277
ISBN 978-1-4331-8808-4 (hardcover)
ISBN 978-1-4331-8809-1 (softcover)
ISBN 978-1-4331-8810-7 (ebook pdf)
ISBN 978-1-4331-8811-4 (epub)
DOI 10.3726/b18349

Dedication

This book is dedicated to Sixth Avenue Clubhouse and Hendersonville Rescue Mission.

Contents

Introduction: The Problem Can Be a Solution

In March 2018, professional basketball player Kevin Love, an All Star power forward for the Cleveland Cavaliers, made an admission on the social media platform Twitter. He never felt comfortable sharing personal information, he told followers, and he previously considered mental health someone else's problem. "I've realized I need to change that," he wrote, sharing an essay he wrote for *The Players' Tribune* titled "Everyone is going through something" (Love, 2018).

The essay, which would propel Love into an unofficial role of mental health spokesman for the National Basketball Association, started by informing readers that he experienced a panic attack in the middle of a basketball game. In 2,500 words, Love walked fans through his experiences with depression and anxiety, the stigmatization of mental health among professional athletes, and how he was inspired to come forward after reading a similar disclosure by fellow NBA star DeMar DeRozan. DeRozan, an All Star for the Toronto Raptors, had written on Twitter, "This depression get the best of me" (DeRozan, 2018), quoting the lyrics of a rap song and generating instant support from the Toronto fanbase.

"Just by sharing what he shared," Love wrote, "DeMar probably helped some people — and maybe a lot more people than we know — feel like they aren't crazy or weird to be struggling with depression. His comments helped take some power away from stigma, and I think that's where the hope is" (Love, 2018, para. 28).

The hope.

Hope might not readily come to mind when one surveys the landscape of mental health in the United States, where people often cannot afford care or find treatment professionals whose calendars bear open slots (e.g., Caron, 2021), and where mental illness remains stigmatized in many communities. Against this backdrop, the disclosure from professional athletes that they, too, at times questioned their worth, struggled with emotional ups and downs, and felt as though they did not belong represented an important moment. Love and DeRozan used the mass media—in this case, social media and an industry magazine—to inspire others to take an initial step toward mental health by talking, sharing, and discussing.

More than 49,000 users retweeted Love's initial post, and the tweet went on to generate international news coverage, disclosures from professional athletes in soccer, football, and other sports, and comments from fans. Since Love's essay appeared in the *Tribune*, the publication has devoted an entire section to mental health. It features more than two dozen essays by elite athletes who share their experiences with substance abuse, depression, anxiety, obsessive compulsive disorder, and other mental health conditions (*The Players' Tribune*, 2022). In addition to inspiring athletes, Love and DeRozan prompted disclosures from fans (Parrott et al., 2020). As one person wrote Love on Twitter, "I might actually go to a counselor now because of this." Another wrote, "Thank you for being a real man and talking about this openly. I am a real man too . . . its (sic) time the stigma stops!"

The growing number of celebrity disclosures may signal an approaching sea change in mass media representations of mental illness. Since the early days of television, people have been concerned about how the mass media represent the subject of mental illness and the people who experience depression, anxiety, schizophrenia, and other disorders. George Gerbner, an influential mass communication researcher, spent time in the 1950s interviewing Hollywood censors to see how they handled the subject of mental illness (Gerbner, 1959). Script writers, he learned, often turned to mental illness when they needed to explain the unexplainable or attribute blame to quickly wrap up mysteries in the condensed format of American television. Censors described themselves as the final barrier blocking writers and producers from bombarding the television-viewing public with exploitive images of mental illness. As one censor put it, "We're holding the line." Another declared, "We are the conscience of the industry" (Gerbner, 1959,

p. 294). Gerbner concluded that "Some 'gatekeepers' go to (and even beyond) the limits of the public relations functions delegated to them in striving for what they consider responsible portrayals. But the methods of censorship are hardly adequate to the task" (p. 303). Indeed, it appears the lines did not hold.

In the 70 years since Gerbner's study, not much changed in the mass media's treatment of mental illness. Media scholars, psychologists, social workers, and mental health advocates have systematically picked apart the content of thousands of television shows, news broadcasts, newspaper articles, cartoons, and movies and found a common caricature of what it means to live with mental illness. Life with mental illness, at least according to the mass media, meant an individual stood greater likelihood than others to attack random strangers or harm themselves. It meant they would live socially excluded existences, devoid of friends, family, or healthy interpersonal relationships. It meant being unemployed, childlike, unable to care for oneself, or sitting in the shadows of a darkened room clutching one's head.

As audience members, we can be affected by the messages we encounter in the mass media. Given the well-documented stereotypes concerning mental illness, people have long expressed concern that the mass media nurture the stigmatization of mental illness by affording people narrow, stereotypical, and inaccurate representations of what it means to have a mental illness. To illustrate, JoAnn A. Thornton and Otto F. Wahl (1996) conducted an experiment in which they exposed a group of participants to a newspaper article in which a person with mental illness committed a violent crime. For another group, the researchers asked participants to first read a counter-stereotypical, "prophylactic" article. The participants who encountered only the stereotypical storyline subsequently reported harsher attitudes toward people with mental illness. Similarly, Donald L. Diefenbach and Mark D. West (2007) studied a week of primetime network television in the United States, finding that characters who were labeled mentally ill stood 10 times greater chance of hurting someone than the rest of the characters who inhabited the TV world. Demonstrating the findings' importance, the researchers examined the relationship between prime-time television exposure and audience members' attitudes toward people with mental illness. People who watched a lot of television were less likely to want mental health facilities in their communities. Beyond public stigma, media stereotypes can also nurture self-stigma among people who experience mental illness. In other words, people might internalize the messages they encounter through the media and feel weird, excluded, or hesitant to seek help because they fear being labeled "mentally ill." They might also feel less self-worth.

In addition to shaping attitudes, media messages guide conversations. To illustrate, a research team in the United States found that online news readers expressed stigmatizing comments when they encountered stories in which people with schizophrenia perpetrated violence (Gwarjanski & Parrott, 2018). "People with psychiatric and/or substance abuse problems should have mandatory treatment and should not be allowed to roam the streets, even if they're not hurting anyone," one reader wrote beneath an online news article. "It's a disgrace."

We see, then, that the concerns expressed by Gerbner's censors in the 1950s lingered into the 1980s, 1990s, 2000s, and modern day, carrying with them the potential for problematic outcomes. Thus, when professional athletes and other successful, popular, and respected people came out via the mass media and said, "I have a mental illness," people listened. People responded.

For some fans, the disclosures represented an impetus for openly talking about mental health, while for others the comments nurtured the desire to seek treatment (Parrott et al., 2020). For scholars, the resulting news coverage and conversations raised questions: At what point do we shift our research focus? At what point do we use research theory and methods to illustrate (and accentuate) the positive effects of mass media exposure on mental health and stigma? At what point do we train our focus toward the positive, the hope Love referenced?

Scientific inquiry should remain objective, and in the area of media studies, scholars should employ sound methodological and theoretical approaches to understanding media content and its effect on individuals and society. Training our scholarly attention toward the potential for positive social change does not represent advocacy. A growing number of researchers are using social scientific approaches to understand how the mass media might have positive effects, rather than negative, on public understanding and appreciation of mental health.

This book seeks to provide readers understanding of the research to date with the hope that it might spark ideas for inquiry, interventions, public relations campaigns, and other "positive" pursuits related to media and stigma. The book combines research in media psychology, social psychology, journalism, public relations, and other fields to better understand how media channels can be used to challenge the stigmatization of mental illness, a social issue that touches everything from politics to prison, education to employment.

Chapter 1 introduces readers to the concept of stigmatization, examining how people have defined the term from the time of ancient Greece, when stigma represented a mark that indicated one's status as a social outcast, to the predominant modern conceptualization in which stigma represents a process of stereotyping, prejudice, and discrimination that occurs within environments of power.

The chapter also discusses research concerning the stigmatization of mental illness in particular.

Building off the literature about stigmatization, Chapter 2 discusses the problematic ways in which the mass media have represented mental illness. It addresses common stereotypes across platforms, discussing the association between mental illness and violence in news stories, movies, television programs, and social media posts.

Chapter 3 marries the earlier chapters, exploring how the mass media might contribute to the stigmatization of mental illness by spreading misinformation, nurturing misunderstanding, and perpetuating discrimination in interpersonal, educational, governmental and other settings.

Our attention shifts to the positive in Chapter 4, which discusses the processes behind the creation of media content. Why are stereotypes common and prevalent across decades and media? Insight can be gleaned through understanding the steps involved in the creation of news stories, movies, and television programs. This understanding, in turn, can provide advocates avenues by which to nurture more accurate representations of mental illness.

Informed by popular mass communication theory, Chapter 5 examines the periods in which the American mass media treat mental health as an important issue, influencing the salience of the subject for the public. The chapter advances recommendations for advocates and others who are interested in seeing mental health higher on the media agenda, and in turn the governmental and public agendas.

As described with the cases of Love and DeRozan, celebrities wield influence over the American public. Chapter 6 examines how celebrities have become important voices in challenging the stigmatization of mental illness, using their platforms to communicate messages to millions in an effort to improve attitudes, reduce prejudice, and challenge discrimination in relation to mental health.

Chapter 7 investigates the prosocial potential for parasocial contact, which occurs when audiences encounter marginalized groups (including people with mental illness) via the mass media.

In Chapter 8, the book explores the ways in which people with mental illness may encounter "kindred spirits" through the mass media, discussing how social media users may connect with others and discuss everything from stigma to therapy, medication to dating.

Protest provides the foundation for Chapter 9, which explains how directly challenging stereotypes, prejudice, and discrimination through the mass media may help mitigate stigma.

Meanwhile, Chapter 10 focuses on the third major approach to challenging stigma—education—and how lessons in media and mental health literacy can help media consumers be more critical of the content they encounter on television, movies, social media and other platforms.

Media technology is omnipresent in modern society, and Chapter 11 examines how virtual reality and video games are permitting people to digitally "walk a mile in the shoes" of a person with mental illness.

Researchers have focused much attention to television, film, and social media, but one of the most popular forms of media entertainment—music—remains under examined. Chapter 12 explores how musicians, from rappers to country music stars, are weaving stories of mental health into their lyrics and molding how new generations understand depression, anxiety, and other illness.

Where do we go from here? Chapter 13 examines this question, providing recommendations for mental health advocates and others who are interested in using the mass media to improve public understanding, attitudes, and behavior related to mental health.

As described in this book, scholars, mental health activists, psychologists and others need not focus on the negative when it comes to media and mental illness. There is abundant opportunity for scholarship—and interventions—focusing on how the problem can be turned into a solution.

References

Caron, C. (2021). 'Nobody has openings' Mental health providers struggle to meet demand. The New York Times. https://www.nytimes.com/2021/02/17/well/mind/therapy-appointments-shortages-pandemic.html

DeRozan, D. (2018). This depression get the best of me. Tweet. https://twitter.com/demar_derozan/status/964818383303688197

Diefenbach, D. L., & West, M. D. (2007). Television and attitudes toward mental health issues: Cultivation analysis and the third-person effect. *Journal of Community Psychology, 35*(2), 181–195.

Gerbner, G. (1959). Mental illness on television: A study of censorship. *Journal of Broadcasting, 3*, 293–303.

Gwarjanski, A. R., & Parrott, S. (2018). Schizophrenia in the news: The role of news frames in shaping online reader dialogue about mental illness. *Health Communication, 33*(8), 954–961.

Love, K. (2018). Everyone is going through something. *The Players' Tribune.* https://www.theplayerstribune.com/articles/kevin-love-everyone-is-going-through-something

Parrott, S., Billings, A. C., Hakim, S. D., & Gentile, P. (2020). From# endthestigma to# realman: Stigma-challenging social media responses to NBA players' mental health disclosures. Communication Reports, *33*(3), 148–160.

Players' Tribune. (2022). Mental health awareness. https://www.theplayerstribune.com/collections/mental-health-awareness

Thornton, J. A., & Wahl, O. F. (1996). Impact of a newspaper article on attitudes toward mental illness. *Journal of Community Psychology, 24*(1), 17–25.

1 When We Talk about Stigma

In the early 2000s, a team of reporters in North Carolina produced two dozen stories about the state's beleaguered mental health system, which fell on hard times during the transition from institutional to community-based care. There were too few private providers, too many people seeking treatment. Crisis care often involved police officers placing a person in the back of a patrol car and transporting them hours to the nearest state institution.

The reporters interviewed parents who lost children to suicide, people unsure where to find help, and administrators trapped in the red tape of bureaucracy. One afternoon, the director of a residential community for people with severe mental illness pulled reporters aside and thanked them for the newspaper's humanizing coverage. It wasn't the usual, she said: "One of the most challenging things about mental illness is stigma, and one of the most challenging things about stigma is the media."

Stigma.

The word was once uncommon outside of gardening and botany books, and indeed Google Books suggests this is one of the primary ways stigma has been used since the 1800s—to describe the tall, central part of a flower that receives pollen. There is also a religious reference, the root of the term stigmata from

Christianity, bodily marks that correspond with the wounds Jesus Christ suffered in the Crucifixion on Galgotha.

But the director was referencing a different type of stigma, one that led people to feel marginalized, stereotyped, and cast aside by families, friends, and communities. It led people to avoid seeking help for fear of being labeled mentally ill, to question whether they could live normal lives with a romantic partner and good job. It was the type of stigma that dated back to ancient Greece, when people were tattooed or marked to communicate their status as social outcasts, slaves, prisoners. People to avoid.

When modern scholars discuss stigma, they often reference the work of Erving Goffman, who described stigma as a delegitimizing mark that resembled, in part, the ancient mark that someone was "a blemished person, ritually polluted, to be avoided, especially in public places" (Goffman, 1997, p. 131). In 1963, Goffman published his seminal book *Stigma: Notes On the Management of a Spoiled Identity*, in which the famed sociologist described stigma as an attribute that devalues a human being in the eyes of society. This definition of stigma now represents the most prevalent usage in modern culture, one whose commonality in everyday conversation and research literature grew in the last 30 years[1]. It also represents the subject of this book.

Stigma is a significant challenge to mental health. People might remain tight-lipped about depression with family and friends, they might have trouble finding treatment because private providers cannot stay in business due to a lack of public funding and insurance parity. Stigma takes different shapes and sizes, rearing its head in educational, employment, healthcare, and social settings. Still, the community director in North Carolina echoed scholars, advocates, and researchers as she expressed optimism that the script could be flipped and mass media could actually represent an important tool in challenging, rather than nurturing, stigma. Toward this end, the chapters of this book describe a budding line of research in which social scientists have sought to understand how exposure to stories—fact and fiction—can change public beliefs, emotions, and attitudes concerning mental illness. To challenge stigma, though, we must first share common understanding of what the term means.

1 To illustrate, the *Journal of Mental Health* published zero articles referencing the term stigma between 1980 and 1990, according to a search of its database. It published 58 articles between 1991 and 2000, 184 articles between 2001 and 2010, and 315 articles between 2011 and 2020.

"A profound barrier"

Scholars have called stigma "one of the most profound barriers to the full social inclusion and community participation of persons with mental illness," and "a powerful process of social control" (Krupa et al., 2009, p. 413). Goffman recommended we approach stigma using "a language of relationships," because an attribute could threaten the identity of one person while strengthening the identity of another. To illustrate, stigmatizing a person with bipolar disorder not only lowers the person in the eyes of the world but reinforces what should be considered normal, providing social backing to the people who belong to the dominant group.

Goffman identified three types of stigma, including abominations of the body, blemishes of character, and tribal stigmas associated with race, nation, and religion. Similar to the ancient marks of Greece, "an individual who might have been received easily in ordinary social intercourse possesses a trait that can obtrude itself upon attention and turn those of us whom he meets away from him" (Goffman, 1997, p. 132).

Modern definitions focus on a process rather than a simple mark. Researchers often reference two definitions of stigma that treat the phenomenon as complex and multi-layered. In the approach of Patrick Corrigan and colleagues, who specialize in psychology, stigmatization is a process in which an individual experiences labeling, stereotypes, prejudice, and discrimination on the basis of a group to which he/she belongs (e.g., Corrigan & Watson, 2002). Labeling occurs when an individual is classified as belonging to a social group, similar to the mark described by Goffman. Labels are ever-present in mental health, where diagnoses are classified and applied using labels: bipolar disorder, depression, anxiety, etc.

Labels call to mind stereotypes, which are characteristics commonly associated with the label. Stereotypes can be positive or negative, but in the case of stigma, they often carry negative connotations. To illustrate, the label "military veteran" can call to mind seemingly positive attributes such as "heroism" or "honor." Conversely, it might also elicit generally negative associations, such as "PTSD" and a propensity for violence (Parrott et al., 2021).

Stereotypes are a precursor to prejudice, or a negative attitude, and prejudice informs discrimination, which is negative behavior. For example, imagine a college student named Holt, who served in the Army. Holt is pursuing his bachelor's degree in marketing when one day, during a group project, he mentions to the other students that he served in the armed forces. The other students would think about Holt as a veteran, and the term could then call to mind positive stereotypes—heroism—and negative stereotypes—post traumatic stress disorder—associated with military veterans. The negative stereotype might cloud a classmate's attitude toward Holt because she associates PTSD with violent behavior. The next time the class divvies into groups, she might avoid associating with Holt (discriminating against him).

The second common definition for stigma was offered by Bruce G. Link and Jo C. Phelan (2001), sociologists who stress the importance of social power in stigma. People who are stigmatized experience labeling, stereotypes, prejudice, and discrimination, but the experience, they argue, must occur within an environment in which the stigmatized person is disenfranchised or lacks power. Building off the previous example, if Holt suddenly found himself unable to identify group members, and therefore less able to succeed in the class, he could be experiencing a loss of power on the basis of labeling, stereotypes, prejudice, and discrimination.

Types and Outcomes of Stigma

Given its social construction, the conditions people stigmatize vary by culture and time period (Major & O'Brien, 2005). Still, research suggests mental illness is stigmatized around the world, and researchers have identified stereotypes about mental illness in media products from the United States, United Kingdom, Canada, the Philippines, China, and other countries. For example, online news outlets in China often write about schizophrenia in relation to violence, publishing headlines such as "Killing mother for trivial matters, schizophrenic man forced to treatment," (Yang & Parrott, 2018, p. 567). Similarly, in the United Kingdom, Matt Bowen and colleagues (2019) analyzed the linguistic characteristics of national newspaper stories about schizophrenia and found the publications often associated schizophrenia and violence. Scholars suggest stigma could be the product of evolution, as it would benefit humans at times to exclude people who are believed to be socially undesirable, diseased, or possessing an unwanted attribute—such as a propensity for violent behavior. When it comes to mental illness, researchers have identified at least four types of stigma: public stigma, self-stigma, stigma by association, and structural stigma.

Public Stigma

Public stigma is "the reaction that the general population has to people with mental illness" (Corrigan & Watson, 2002). It includes negative stereotypes that associate mental illness with incompetence, weakness, and/or dangerousness (Rüsch et al., 2005). It occurs when an individual endorses those stereotypes and demonstrates prejudice and discrimination toward a person with mental illness. Recalling our earlier example, the military veteran Holt experienced public stigma when classmates treated him differently because they associated him with PTSD and danger.

Public stigma can be problematic for both the individual and society. For example, let's say a mental health organization wants to build a new halfway house in an area of town known for its tree-lined sidewalks, historic houses, and award-winning elementary school. A homeowners' association hears about the plan for the home and protests, effectively saying "not in our backyard" based on stereotypes about mental illness. For another example, imagine the veteran Holt seeking employment to help cover housing and other expenses while he works toward his marketing degree. The manager of a local department store questions whether Holt would be good in sales because he assumes Holt has anger control issues.

These examples are not far from reality, as researchers have found that public stigma creates negative outcomes for people with mental illness in housing, educational, employment, romantic, and other settings. People might avoid an individual who has mental illness, which can lead the person to feel isolated and alone (worsening their illness). Citizens might support coercive treatment approaches, such as forced medication compliance. They might also support segregation, expressing preference for institutionalized rather than community-based mental health care (Corrigan & Watson, 2002). Work, which can nurture mental health, might also suffer because of stigma. Coworkers or employers might express prejudice toward mental illness in general or specifically target an individual. Policies can be put in place that are outdated and neglect mental health, such as with leave policies or health insurance (e.g., Stuart, 2006). People might attempt to maintain privacy among coworkers and employers, creating pressure as they worry whether their condition will be discovered (Krupa et al., 2009). Assumptions abound: A person with serious mental illness could never work; employers can focus on disabilities rather than abilities, threatening chances for promotion; people with mental illness are dangerous and unpredictable, and therefore a liability in the workplace (Krupa et al., 2009).

Perhaps it is not surprising, given these outcomes, that stigma has been identified as a significant barrier to mental health. People might avoid treatment for fear of being labeled "mentally ill" and experiencing the associated stigma. They might discontinue treatment after perceiving prejudice or discrimination. Indeed, even medical professionals—to whom a person turns for help—can stigmatize mental illness, presenting potential barriers to treatment (e.g., Papish et al., 2013).

Self-stigma

Self-stigma occurs when a person who experiences mental illness endorses stereotypes about the condition, resulting in threatened or reduced self-esteem or self-efficacy (Major & O'Brien, 2005). This could translate into negative outcomes such as avoiding mental health treatment or the pursuit of employment (Rüsch et al., 2005). A person might also experience fear or stereotype threat when they believe others are looking at them through the lens of negative stereotypes. The idea is in line with Goffman's (1997) description of a stigmatized person never knowing what others really think while being overly cognizant of the impression they are making. Such thinking can be problematic because it eats up cognitive resources, potentially throwing off our interactions and ability to concentrate. It might also feed into stereotype threat, which happens when we live up to stereotypes because we are so preoccupied by the stereotype it interferes with our thinking. To illustrate, a famous social psychology study found that White people were worse at golf when it was described as a game of "natural athletic ability." Meanwhile, Black participants played worse golf when the game was described as a test of "sports intelligence" (Stone et al., 1999). The mass media might play an important role in self-stigma, as Corrigan (2004, p. 618) notes that "living in a culture steeped in stigmatizing images, persons with mental illness may accept these notions and suffer diminished self-esteem, self-efficacy, and confidence in one's future."

Stigma by Association

Stigma by association occurs when an individual becomes discredited because they are a family member, friend, or close acquaintance with a stigmatized person. Stigma by association may be especially problematic for family members. Parents (especially mothers) might be blamed for causing or worsening a child's mental illness. A child's social relationships might be severed when a parent experiences mental illness. Meanwhile, a sibling might lose friends or feel pressure to schedule social dates around the presence of a brother or sister with mental illness. Such findings were documented by Remko van der Sanden, a researcher in the Netherlands, who interviewed 23 family members of people with mental illness to better understand whether (and how) they experienced stigma by association (2013). In another study, this time with 503 people whose family members had mental illness, van der Sanden and colleagues (2016) found that family members' experiences with stigma by association predicted heightened psychological distress and lower quality of life, especially when family members lacked adaptive coping strategies.

Structural Stigma

A final type of stigma involves the structures of our society. Institutions, from schools to legal systems, stigmatize through the implementation of laws or policies that disenfranchise people with mental illness and their families. In 2015, a team of researchers at Columbia University released a commissioned report on structural stigma and mental illness for the National Academy of Sciences, Engineering and Medicine (Pugh et al., 2015). Although interpersonal stigma is more common, the researchers reported, it functions within the context of structural stigma. Structural stigma includes discriminatory legislation, which was documented in all 50 states in relation to mental illness. Many of the laws limit the rights of people with mental illness, including limitations on voting, firearms, holding political office, serving on juries, etc. Laws often use the broad umbrella term of mental illness rather than taking into account factors such as cognitive or functional impairment. As the team reported, "such arbitrariness is the defining feature of structural stigma and reflects the stereotype that all (people with mental illness) are dangerous or inadequate in some way and therefore deserving of fewer liberties and opportunities" (p. 3). Structural stigma may also manifest itself in "paternalism, reduced expectations, heightened scrutiny and coercion (that) are embedded in many public agencies and service structures," the report states.

The Building Blocks of Stigma

As noted, modern definitions of stigma describe a process involving labeling, stereotyping, prejudice, and discrimination within environments of power.

Labeling

We, as humans, label. Labels help us identify objects ("There is a chair") and signal attributes of the objects ("There is a broken chair"). Labels convey information that might be useful ("If you sit on a broken chair, you will fall"), and in evolutionary settings, labels have helped us identify friends and foes, threats and rewards.

When it comes to the social world, labels can carry an alternative—and darker—application. Labels can convey difference, divvying the world into "us" and "them" and providing the foundation for stereotypes, prejudice, and discrimination based upon the way we look, the God we worship, the money we make, our mental health, or any number other attributes. In the context of stigma, labeling occurs when people are designated as representing a group, attribute, or behavior that is considered undesirable within a social context (Major & O'Brien, 2005).

A label can be conferred by oneself ("I am depressed") or someone else, such as a psychiatrist diagnosing a patient with clinical depression (Corrigan, 2004). Labels might also be inferred, such as when a person is seen walking out of a therapist's office and assumed to be mentally ill (Corrigan, 2004). Labeling implies "that 'they' are fundamentally different from 'us' and that 'they' even are the thing they are labelled" (Rusch et al., 2005, p. 530). A number of cues may signal that someone warrants the label of mentally illness, including explicit terms ("He's depressed"), physical differences, deficits in social skills, or actual psychiatric symptoms (Corrigan, 2004). Labels are the first step in the stigma process, calling to mind assumptions about what we might expect from the person who has been classified. These assumptions are called stereotypes.

Stereotyping

We are bombarded by information each day. Our minds are working away as we eat breakfast, commute to work, converse with colleagues, and scroll through social media. Most of us do not worry about actual survival the way our ancestors did, anticipating threats or rewards to survive another day, but the mental shortcuts they passed down to us over the generations can be helpful. Stereotypes represent such cognitive shortcuts, associations quickly called to mind when we meet people who belong to different social groups.

Let us say while walking down the street one day, you encounter a man wearing rags and begging for change. Based on your life experiences (and even those from TV), your mind should quickly process the scene and call to mind certain words, images, and emotions (such as homeless, poor, sadness, fear). The stereotypes can inform your subsequent attitudes and behavior: Do you donate food, money? Do you cross the street to avoid the man, reach into your pocket for pepper spray, try to help?

Labels can quickly trigger assumptions in our minds, which can affect our attitudes and behavior, sometimes even beyond our own conscious awareness. Stereotypes are "social knowledge structures that pre-determine our attitudes" (Arboleda-Florez, 2002, p. 26). While scientists have much to learn about the human brain, memory has been described as a network of connected concepts. When one concept is primed, the activation spreads to nearby concepts, activating them for use. The more strongly the concepts are associated, the more likely they are to be activated in concert, affecting subsequent perceptions and behavior.

To illustrate, students at the University of Alabama often use the phrase "Roll Tide" to show support for the football team, passing exams, greeting passers-by, or simply waking up to pretty weather. In seminars, I begin a section on media priming by telling students, "I am going to say a word, and I want you to tell me what first comes to mind." I say the word "Roll," and almost in concert, they immediately respond with "Tide." For these students, the association between the concepts of "Roll" and "Tide" have been reinforced through consistent, frequent use. In comparison, when I say the word "Roll" to students from Oregon or Montana, they are more likely to think of dinner or toilet paper. While colloquial phrases are not stereotypes, the example illustrates the way in which stereotypes about social groups work, and how we can be conditioned to think certain things about certain people. If you are walking down the street and overhear a person talking to himself, you might think "mentally ill," *labeling* the person, which could then trigger an increased perception of danger or threat, a *stereotype*. Stereotypes also have affective components. In other words, your experience might elicit an emotion such as fear. While stereotypes help us navigate the world, they can also be problematic, nurturing prejudice and discrimination. People who belong to a stereotyped group might also come to believe a stereotype, experiencing threatened self-esteem and self-efficacy.

The mass media play an important role in communicating and reinforcing stereotypes. Scholars have documented stereotypes concerning race, gender, age, and mental illness on the evening news, primetime programming, and even Saturday morning cartoons (see Billings & Parrott, 2020). Chapter 2 illustrates how the mass media have traditionally stereotyped mental illness, associating it with violence and social failure. The more viewers encounter stereotypes, the stronger the associations become in their minds and the more readily they can be summoned in later social situations (e.g., Major & O'Brien, 2005). People probably stand an increased likelihood of calling to mind negative thoughts about mentally ill people when their media diet features "maniac" cartoon characters, crime TV shows in which imaginary voices tell a man to hold people hostage, news stories about a mass murderer with autism, and political debates in which presidential candidates call one another "nuts" and "crazy."

Prejudice

Stereotypes can be automatically activated, which means anyone—including those who are not prejudiced—might readily call to mind negative thoughts about other social groups because of the messages they encounter in the media, the communities in which they live, the family members they grow up around. A person demonstrates explicit prejudice when they endorse those stereotypes (Corrigan & Watson, 2002), saying "Yes, people are cowards when they have anxiety all the time," or "Yes, only weak people experience depression."

Prejudice is an attitude, or an evaluation of an object or, in this case, a characteristic. People express prejudice through words or agreement with thoughts. We also express our prejudice through emotions such as anger, hate, and fear. At times we are cognizant of our prejudice. In the context of mental illness, for example, a person might think, "Yes, people with schizophrenia are dangerous." At other times we might not even be aware of our negative attitude, a phenomenon called implicit prejudice. For example, Cheryl L. Dickter and colleagues (2021) gauged parents' implicit attitudes toward children with autism before exposure to autism-related educational resources from *Sesame Street*, the generations-old public television show for children. One week after exposing parents to the television program, the research team re-assessed the parents' implicit attitudes, measured based on the speed with which parents associated positive (e.g., marvelous) and negative (e.g., terrible) terms with autistic children. Researchers grouped parents into two categories for analysis—those who had a child with autism, and those who did not—and they found that parents without autistic children expressed greater implicit bias than parents whose children had autism in the initial test. In the second test, after exposure to *Sesame Street*, the implicit attitudes no longer significantly differed, suggesting the television program had a dampening effect on parents' prejudice.

Discrimination

As with prejudice, discrimination may occur intentionally or unintentionally. Building off the earlier example of the homeless man, crossing the street to avoid a feeling of danger would represent discrimination, even if you did not think through the behavior. A number of the negative outcomes of mental illness stigma are examples of discrimination. For example, American prisons are heavily populated by people with mental illness, leading one politician to describe the penal system as "the defacto mental health system." The overrepresentation is the byproduct of what Corrigan (2004) called "criminalizing mental illness," which occurs when a person in crisis is arrested instead of provided treatment. In addition to thoughts, our emotions can drive discrimination. For example, fear could lead an employer to avoid hiring a person with mental illness, while anger could lead to replacing health care with jail (Corrigan & Watson, 2002). These latter examples illustrate the dynamic of power in stigma.

Power

Bruce Link and Jo Phelan (2014) highlight the significance of power in stigma, writing that stigma performs three functions within social hierarchy: it keeps people down, in, and away. The process of keeping people away, they write, reflects the original idea of stigma as a mark to separate healthy from unhealthy, fit from unfit. Stigma also keeps people down, because "wealth, power, and high social status can be attained when one group dominates or exploits another" they write (p. 2). Finally, stigma "keeps people in" by communicating and reinforcing social norms, or the rules we follow concerning appropriate beliefs, attitudes, and behavior within society. All three functions reinforce symbolic power, but Link and Phelan perceive the latter motivation as the initial reason for mental illness stigma, as a person recognizes having a condition that is stigmatized and attempts to follow cultural norms and stay "in." As mental illness symptoms progress, the motivation behind stigma transitions into keeping people down and away. The process begins with a "cultural assessment of value," in which a person with mental illness recognizes the societal value (or lack of value) placed in people who experience mental illness.

Mental health advocates could argue that the mass media are one instrument by which people become aware of the cultural devaluation regarding people with mental illness. Indeed, this was essentially the statement of the mental health director in North Carolina.

Was she correct? Have the media done a poor job informing the public about mental illness?

The answer, it turns out, is a resounding yes.

References

Arboleda-Florez, J. (2002). What causes stigma?. *World Psychiatry, 1*(1), 25.

Arboleda-Flórez, J. (2003). Considerations on the stigma of mental illness. *The Canadian Journal of Psychiatry, 48*(10), 645–650.

Billings, A., Parrott, S. (2020). *Media Stereotypes: From Ageism to Xenophobia*. Peter Lang.

Bos, A. E., Pryor, J. B., Reeder, G. D., & Stutterheim, S. E. (2013). Stigma: Advances in theory and research. *Basic and Applied Social Psychology, 35*(1), 1–9.

Bowen, M., Kinderman, P., & Cooke, A. (2019). Stigma: A linguistic analysis of the UK red-top tabloids press' representation of schizophrenia. *Perspectives in Public Health, 139*(3), 147–152.

Corrigan, P. (2004). How stigma interferes with mental health care. *American Psychologist, 59*(7), 614.

Corrigan, P. W., & Kleinlein, P. (2005). *The impact of mental illness stigma*. In P. W. Corrigan (Ed.), On the stigma of mental illness: Practical strategies for research and social change (pp. 11–44). American Psychological Association.

Corrigan, P. W., & Watson, A. C. (2002). Understanding the impact of stigma on people with mental illness. *World Psychiatry, 1*(1), 16.

Dickter, C. L., Burk, J. A., Anthony, L. G., Robertson, H. A., Verbalis, A., Seese, S., . . . & Anthony, B. J. (2021). Assessment of *Sesame Street* online autism resources: Impacts on parental implicit and explicit attitudes toward children with autism. *Autism, 25*(1), 114–124.

Goffman, E. (1997). Selections from *Stigma*. *The Disability Studies Reader, 203*, 215.

Link, B. G., & Phelan, J. C. (2001). Conceptualizing stigma. *Annual Review of Sociology, 27*(1), 363–385.

Link, B. G., & Phelan, J. C. (2006). Stigma and its public health implications. *The Lancet, 367*(9509), 528–529.

Link, B. G., & Phelan, J. C. (2013). Labeling and stigma. In C. S. Aneshensel, J. C. Phelan, & A. Bierman (Eds.), *Handbook of the sociology of mental health* (pp. 525–541). Springer.

Link, B. G., & Phelan, J. (2014). Stigma power. *Social Science & Medicine, 103*, 24–32.

Major, B., & O'Brien, L. T. (2005). The social psychology of stigma. *Annual Review of Psychology, 56*, 393–421.

Papish, A., Kassam, A., Modgill, G., Vaz, G., Zanussi, L., & Patten, S. (2013). Reducing the stigma of mental illness in undergraduate medical education: A randomized controlled trial. *BMC Medical Education, 13*(1), 1–10.

Pescosolido, B. A., & Martin, J. K. (2015). The stigma complex. *Annual Review of Sociology, 41*, 87–116.

Pugh, T., Hatzenbuehler, M., & Link, B. (2015). Structural stigma and mental illness. Commissioned Paper for Committee on the Science of Changing Behavioural Health Social Norms, Mailman School of Public, Columbia University (August 2015).

Rüsch, N., Angermeyer, M. C., & Corrigan, P. W. (2005). Mental illness stigma: Concepts, consequences, and initiatives to reduce stigma. *European Psychiatry, 20*(8), 529–539.

Stone, J., Lynch, C. I., Sjomeling, M., & Darley, J. M. (1999). Stereotype threat effects on Black and White athletic performance. *Journal of Personality and Social Psychology, 77*(6), 1213.

van der Sanden, R. L., Bos, A. E., Stutterheim, S. E., Pryor, J. B., & Kok, G. (2013). Experiences of stigma by association among family members of people with mental illness. *Rehabilitation Psychology, 58*(1), 73–80.

van der Sanden, R. L., Pryor, J. B., Stutterheim, S. E., Kok, G., & Bos, A. E. (2016). Stigma by association and family burden among family members of people with mental illness: The mediating role of coping. *Social Psychiatry and Psychiatric Epidemiology, 51*(9), 1233–1245.

Yang, Y., & Parrott, S. (2018). Schizophrenia in Chinese and US online news media: Exploring cultural influence on the mediated portrayal of schizophrenia. *Health Communication, 33*(5), 553–561.

2

A History of Violence: Mental Illness in the Media

In 2012, a gunman murdered 12 people in a movie theater in Aurora, Colorado. The man confessed to the crime but pleaded not guilty by reason of insanity. The violent act—and the man's trial three years later—generated international news stories, attention-grabbing headlines, and comments from pundits on social media who called for gun control, the death penalty, and coercive treatment for people with mental illness. Beneath one article, a reader opined, "Insane people walking around free and untreated never cause any harm to anyone, just ask those folks in the theatr (sic) in colorado (sic), or ask Gabby Giffords, she will tell you" (Gwarjanski & Parrott, 2018), referencing additional instances of violence.

The public outrage is understandable, given innocent men, women, and children died simply because they wanted to watch a new super hero movie. However, the 24–7 media coverage and pontification by armchair experts represent a problem facing mental health. When journalists write about mental illness, the stories usually do not concern education, medical breakthroughs, or humanizing narratives in which a person talks about what it means to live with mental illness. Instead, conditions such as schizophrenia most often arise as a secondary conversation to an act of extreme violence (Gwarjanski & Parrott, 2018). A search of Google News for stories with the term "schizophrenia" returned tabloid headlines such as "Off to the gym: The schizophrenic, 28, who used a screwdriver to kill an expectant mother the last time he was out alone" (Daily Mail, 2022), and "Mind of a Monster: I was driven to kill by 'the voice'" (Asbury Park-Press, 2022).

Such stories are nothing new. Indeed, scholars have documented stereotypes about mental illness in mass media since the dawn of television 70 years ago, when network censors bemoaned scriptwriters' exploitation of mental illness for shock value and horror (Gerbner, 1959). Movies, television shows, news articles, and even children's cartoons perpetuate stereotypes about mental illness, describing characters as "nuts" and "wacko," blaming violence squarely on mental illness, and portraying love as the most effective approach for lifting a struggling person from the pits of despair (Owen, 2012; Parrott, 2020).

The representations are problematic because they potentially feed stigma. Indeed, the mass media represent a prominent source of information about mental health for many people. Stigma can create a vicious cycle. People may be unwilling to openly talk about mental health, sharing personal experience or positive comments about treatment, leading people to incorrectly assume they know no one who has experienced depression, anxiety, bipolar disorder, or another condition. The silence creates an information void into which the omnipresent media might step, sharing falsehoods about symptoms, treatments, outlooks, and who can be affected by mental illness. As this chapter illustrates, tropes about mental illness persist over time, cut across cultures, and appear everywhere from Twitter to TV.

In the News . . .

Check out news websites, and the portrait you find of mental illness is often one featuring violence, exclusion, and questionable medical practices.

"It always comes down to mental illness," according to an opinion piece on Fox News, the most viewed television news station in the United States. "Take all the guns away. Take all the knives away. The number of victims of murders with no apparent motive—born of undertreated, poorly treated, or untreated mental illness—will be reduced not one bit" (Ablow, 2015). Meanwhile, in health news, Reuters reported, "Millions of healthy people — including shy or defiant children, grieving relatives and people with fetishes — may be wrongly labeled mentally ill by a new international diagnostic manual, specialists said on Thursday" (Reuters, 2015). The stories embody the traditional approach journalists have taken while covering covering the subject of mental illness, approaching the topic in two contexts: while covering the crime beat, or while conducting exposés on the nation's mental health systems. One approach elicits anger, the other pity. Both approaches feed stigma.

Since the 1970s, researchers have found consistent themes while studying the representation of mental illness in American news media. First, journalists have been criticized for primarily quoting expert sources—doctors, family members—rather than people who experience mental illness. Second, journalists often cover stories that associate mental illness with violent and unpredictable behavior, though coverage may be shifting to include more news on health and science. Third, news sites traditionally lacked educational information about mental health, such as the causes and symptoms of different disorders. Fourth, journalists represent people with mental illness as unable to care for themselves or as victims of everything from bureaucratic red tape to abuse.

To illustrate, Anna Rae Gwarjanski systematically examined how traditional news organizations—such as *The New York Times* and *Washington Post*—and digital-native websites—*Buzzfeed*, *Gawker*—covered the subject of schizophrenia in stories over the course of one year. Digital-native websites are increasingly common in modern media, as news organizations skip the process of print publishing and instead embrace social media and websites. Gwarjanski wondered whether the digital sites would buck tradition and publish more helpful articles about schizophrenia when compared to their predecessors, the self-proclaimed publishers of "all the news that's fit to print." She examined 558 articles to see how often the publications published stigmatizing stories or stigma-challenging stories (Gwarjanski & Parrott, 2018). She also examined reader comments that were posted beneath the articles to see what kind of online conversations the stories generated.

In the end, Gwarjanski found that the traditional news outlets often wrote about schizophrenia only when referencing crimes such as the mass shooting in Colorado. In contrast, *Buzzfeed* and other digital native sites shared news about scientific breakthroughs, medical innovations, and even personal essays written by people who were affected by schizophrenia. The difference in reader dialogue was striking: People disclosed their own experiences and shared empathy-inducing testimonials beneath the stigma-challenging stories. The stigmatizing stories, meanwhile, elicited angry and hateful comments from readers who wanted to see people with mental illness locked away.

Despite the focus on schizophrenia, the stories rarely quoted people who had experienced mental illness. Overall, one in five of the articles quoted an individual with mental illness. The finding illustrates the concerns of mental health advocates who claim that journalists rarely interview people who have experienced mental illness, instead quoting elite sources such as medical professionals and government officials.

Indeed, another study reached comparable conclusions after examining stories related to the inclusion of gaming disorder in psychological diagnostic manuals (Parrott et al., 2020). Gaming disorder, which focuses on problematic use of video games, generated controversy when it was first discussed for inclusion in the diagnostic manuals of the American Psychiatric Association and the World Health Organization. While covering the controversy, journalists gravitated toward researchers, medical professionals, and gaming industry officials when discussing the controversy. Journalists rarely quoted gamers, the people who would actually be affected by the condition. Such exclusion from the public record led one person to tell Raymond G. Nairn and John H. Coverdale (2005) that "People never see us living well." Nairn and Coverdale dissected 600 news stories about mental illness in New Zealand and discovered that only 5 articles (less than 1%) reported directly on the experiences of a person with mental illness. In these rare examples, journalists permitted the sources to talk about their experience with stigma, describe doing typical things in life (such as cooking, cleaning), and also talk about their experiences with mental disorders and treatment. Such representations present more well-rounded and humanizing portraits of mental illness than stories focusing on violence and instability.

Patrick Corrigan and colleagues describe newspaper articles as measures of structural stigma, which is "formed by sociopolitical forces and represents policies of private and government institutions that restrict the opportunities of the groups that are stigmatized" (2005, p. 551). His research team examined 3,353 stories about mental illness that were drawn from six one-week periods in 2002 from major newspapers in the United States. Nearly 4 in 10 stories (39%) featured violence and dangerousness. In addition to stereotypes, people often misunderstand the causes and symptoms of mental disorders. Given this concern, the research team also examined how journalists presented the causes of mental disorders, finding that they predominantly focused on genetic, biological, or environmental causes, rather than blaming the person or their family for the illness (a positive finding). One in five articles, meanwhile, shared information related to advocacy, focusing on the need for better care, mental health resources, housing, and insurance parity.

Interestingly, stereotypes are common across countries. In the United Kingdom, for example, researcher Matt Bowen examined how newspapers represented mental illness in word choice, news stories, and the social media platform Twitter. Bowen (2019) used linguistic analysis to examine a decade of popular press stories and found they, too, often focused on violence when discussing personality disorders. In 2020, Bowen and colleagues illustrated the importance of studying media representations of specific disorders, rather than the umbrella terms "mental illness" or "mental disorders." In this study, the research team studied how the popular press in the UK represented anorexia nervosa on Twitter. Culture perpetuates different stereotypes about anorexia than schizophrenia, which is often associated with violence. For example, anorexia and other conditions related to body image are often stereotyped as "women's illnesses," which might lead to stigma for men who experience the disorder and need treatment (Parrott et al., 2022). Bowen and colleagues conducted a thematic analysis of 332 news stories from national newspapers in the UK. The researchers identified four themes, each of which performed Entman's (1993) functions of news frames (i.e., defining problems, identifying causes, describing consequences, recommending treatments, and presenting moral evaluations). News organizations often focused on the role of social factors in placing pressure on people in terms of body appearance. Stories also advanced a second theme—an illness model—in which people called on anorexia being viewed as an illness. Less common, but problematic, were stories that followed a "clickbait model" in which journalists used sexualized images of underweight women that were designed to "elicit a response of fascinated horror" (p. 134).

On the Big Screen . . .

Norman Bates is perhaps the most famous embodiment of mental illness in American film, a mild mannered inn keeper who dresses as his dead mother and murders guests in the Alfred Hitchcock film *Psycho.* By no means, though, is Bates alone. He represents a trope in American film, a murderous person whose behavior is explained as mental illness. Much the same as news media, the representation of mental illness in film has long been problematic. Stereotypes are so common that advocacy groups such as the National Alliance on Mental Illness established letter writing campaigns and protests to be on the lookout for movies that perpetuate stereotypes about mental illness.

Problematic representations are not relegated to movies from bygone years. For example, the movie *Me, Myself and Irene* was released in theaters in 2000. The film featured popular comedian Jim Carrey in the lead role, a law enforcement officer who develops "advanced delusionary schizophrenia with involuntary narcissistic rage." Carrey's character shifts between the two personalities, one of which is meek and kind, the other violent and angry. The National Alliance on Mental Illness protested the film, challenging the representation of schizophrenia as split personality as inaccurate and its focus on violence as stereotypical. The film also generated outrage because it used mental illness for comedic purposes, and used offensive language such as "schizo" (Byrne, 2000).

Patricia R. Owen (2012) studied cinematic portrayals of schizophrenia between 1990 and 2010, studying how films represented the people affected, symptoms, causes, and treatments. Her team found 42 characters in 41 films. The characters often demonstrated delusional behavior, and a majority of the characters were violent toward themselves or others. Less common were messages concerning the causation and treatment of the disorder.

Stigma is not confined to adult comedies or horror films. At the University of Calgary, researchers Andrea Lawson and Gregory Fouts studied the representation of mental illness in 64 years of Disney films. Disney movies are incredibly popular and influential, reaching millions of children and adults. The seminal nature of the characters (and the marketing machine behind the toys, clothing, and other products they birth) mean the movies stick around for generations: consider *Snow White*, *101 Dalmatians*, *The Lion King*, and *Beauty and the Beast*. After studying 34 films, Lawson and Fouts described the movies' portrayal of mental illness as problematic. 85% of the animated films made reference to mental illness, often using derogatory terms such as "crazy," "mad," "nut," and "nutty." In *Beauty and the Beast*, for example, characters call the protagonist Belle and her father, Maurice, mentally ill because their behavior and attitudes (e.g., valuing books over beauty) do not subscribe to societal norms. In the end, the townspeople carry Maurice away in a horse-drawn wagon with barred windows and the phrase, "Les Maisons des Lunes," or "asylum for loons."

The mass media reflect society. As social attitudes toward mental illness changed, representations on film follow suit—at times. Since the early 2000s, several movies garnered praise for humanizing mental illness. For example, the National Alliance on Mental Illness released a list of films that "get it right," (Greenstein, 2017, para. 2), including *Matchstick Men,* "an honest depiction of the rituals and behaviors of someone living with OCD," and *Silver Linings Playbook*, which "represents the range of emotion that often occurs with bipolar disorder in a real and riveting way."

Still, movies can receive praise while perpetuating problematic stereotypes. *A Beautiful Mind*, released in 2001, portrayed the life of Nobel Prize-winning mathematician John Forbes Nash Jr. as he navigated life with schizophrenia. NAMI featured the film in its list of "best movies about mental health" (Greenstein,

2017), and university professors have used the movie to teach college students about schizophrenia (Rosenstock, 2003). Even this film had its problems, though. Critics contend the film perpetuated a positive stereotype about mental illness, namely that it nurtures uncanny abilities. Owen's (2012) analysis confirmed the presence of positive stereotypes in other films: in her examination of movies featuring schizophrenia, 17% of characters demonstrated special talents or abilities while 12% possessed "visionary insights or paranormal abilities that ostensibly allowed interaction with otherworldly and often malevolent forces" (p. 657).

And the Small Screen . . .

The television show *Criminal Minds* lasted 15 seasons and reached millions of viewers each week in the United States, not counting the millions more viewers it reached through syndication and streaming services. Through the crime drama, viewers follow "an elite team of FBI profilers who analyze the country's most twisted criminal minds, anticipating their next moves before they strike again" (Paramount, 2022). The show became so popular it inspired spin-offs, including *Criminal Minds: Suspect Behavior* and *Criminal Minds: Beyond Borders*, as well as fan websites in which newcomers to the franchise can explore episodes, read about characters, and connect with other fans (Fandom, 2022). The fan site also keeps a running tally on the number of characters diagnosed with schizophrenia, classifying them into categories of "non-criminal" and "criminal." There are 12 criminals on the list, including Rhett Walden Jr., "a necrophilic budding spree killer and abductor who had a schizophrenic hallucination of his mother," and Darrin Call, "a spree killer, one-time cop killer, and one-time abductor whose schizophrenia coupled with severe PTSD from the crimes of his father drove him to go on a killing spree after he couldn't obtain his anti-psychotic medication" (Fandom, 2022). In addition to these fictional killers, the website provides readers examples of "real-world people who have/had schizophrenia," including Theodore Kaczynski (also known as The Unabomber), Ed Kemper (aka, The Co-Ed Killer), and David Berkowitz (aka, Son of Sam).

Despite its outlandish plots, *Criminal Minds* is not necessarily an outlier when it comes to the representation of schizophrenia and other mental illnesses on television. When George Gerbner (1959) interviewed network censors in the early years of TV, they described themselves as the final barrier protecting the masses from scriptwriters' exploitation of mental illness for shock and horror. Decades later, mental illness remains an easy explanation for nefarious behavior in cops-and-robbers television programs. Indeed, recent research reached this conclusion after examining how crime dramas portrayed mental illness in 65 episodes of television programs from 2010 to 2013 (Parrott & Parrott, 2015). The article used a scene from *Criminal Minds: Suspect Behavior* to illustrate how the law-and-order television shows perpetuated stereotypes associating mental illness with violent and criminal behavior. "A young man named Michael loads his dead sister into the front passenger seat of his 1970s American muscle car and barrels down the back-roads of the eastern United States, murdering random strangers along the way by hanging them from tree branches, bridges, and roof beams," the article begins. The crimes stump federal investigators, who cannot determine the motive behind Michael's attacks. When they discover Michael has schizophrenia, the detectives all seem to understand. Ultimately the study found that Michael wasn't traversing the world of crime TV alone in his diagnosis or murderous behavior. Characters who were labeled mentally ill stood greater likelihood of committing crimes and violence than the remaining population of characters, perpetuating stereotypes.

Nancy Signorielli studied 17 years of primetime network television content from the United States and found that the shows often associated mental illness with violence and victimization (1989). Nearly a decade later, Diefenbach (1997) compared violence in the TV world to real-world violence involving people with mental illness. Characters who were mentally ill stood greater chance of perpetrating violence than the rest of the TV population, and they were 10–20 times more violent than people with mental illness in the U.S. population.

Again, stereotypes are not confined to adult programming. Echoing the Disney movie study, Claire Wilson and colleagues (2000) examined how children's television programming in New Zealand represented mental illness. Nearly half of the 128 television episodes (46%) made reference to mental illness, most often cartoons. The shows used terms such as "crazy," "mad," and "losing your mind" to indicate losing control, and the researchers (p. 440) described the programming as "almost entirely devoid of admirable attributes."

Still, television is changing. While empirical data is lacking, commenters have noted an increasing frequency of storylines in which actors educate viewers about mental health and illness. For example, the television comedy *Monk* follows a lovable detective whose career and relationships are affected by obsessive compulsive disorder. Pundits lauded the show for humanizing mental illness. Still, others worried the program would lead the public to oversimplify what it means to live with OCD. Cynthia A. Hoffner and Elizabeth L. Cohen (2018) surveyed 44 people with anxiety disorders to see what they thought about the television program, and responses were mixed. Fans said the show helped challenge stereotypes because it portrayed a person with mental illness as successful in his personal and professional lives. However, critics contended the show perpetuated incorrect beliefs and stereotypes about OCD. One respondent's comment captured the ambivalence toward the program among fans with OCD: "A few of my friends with OCD feel that the humor on the show is a way of mocking Monk, but I strongly disagree — I don't see it as disrespectful at all, and having a sense of humor is healthy and helpful in managing anything, including a mental illness!" (p. 164).

Similarly, the television show *Perception* followed world-renowned neuroscientist Dr. Daniel Pierce as he consults with detectives on complicated criminal cases. The series presented a rounded representation of mental illness by featuring a central character who is largely successful in his profession, friendships, and romantic relationship. The show is not perfect, though, as commenters have described the program as perpetuating the stereotype that associates mental illness with incredible insight.

The proliferation of streaming services—such as HBO Max, Amazon Prime, and Netflix—appears to be leading to an increase in programs centered around mental health (for better or worse). A program on Netflix called *Thirteen Reasons Why* generated controversy in its representation of a teenage protagonist's suicide. Conversely, HBO Max and Netflix released documentaries in which elite athletes openly discussed their experiences with depression, suicidal ideations, anxiety, and other illnesses. *The Weight of Gold,* a documentary produced by HBO and the Olympian Michael Phelps, featured interviews with American athletes who described severe depression and thoughts of suicide after competing in the Olympics. The documentary also demonstrates how stories are no longer appearing on an isolated medium, instead reaching social media, websites, newsprint, and film all at once. Athletes, agents, and mental health advocates advertised *The Weight of Gold* on social media, participated in town hall meetings, and shared their stories with news outlets.

Why Should We Care?

Overall, the mass media have traditionally portrayed people with mental illness as unstable, unpredictable, and threatening—the ingredients for an atmosphere in which people who experience mental illness could be stigmatized. A new generation of scriptwriters, journalists, and content producers may be flipping the script, though, as evidenced by an increasing focus on science and health by journalists and well-rounded characters by screenwriters.

While stereotypes are well-documented in the mass media, researchers have done less work to understand the specific ways exposure to stereotypes affects audience members' beliefs, attitudes, emotions, and behavior related to mental health. The argument certainly stands to reason, and indeed researchers have found that stereotypes of other groups (e.g., race, gender) elicit stereotypical thinking, prejudicial attitudes, and discriminatory behavior toward marginalized groups (see Billings & Parrott, 2020).

In the next chapter, we will discuss how researchers are using surveys, experiments, and other research approaches to understand how exposure to media stereotypes informs everything from attitudes about everything from social relationships to government policy.

References

Ablow, K. (2015). It always comes down to mental illness. Fox News. https://www.foxnews.com/opinion/it-always-comes-down-to-mental-illness

Bowen, M. (2019). Stigma: A linguistic analysis of personality disorder in the UK popular press, 2008–2017. *Journal of Psychiatric and Mental Health Nursing, 26*(7–8), 244–253.

Bowen, M., Lovell, A., & Waller, R. (2020). Stigma: The representation of anorexia nervosa in UK newspaper Twitter feeds. *Journal of Mental Health*, 1–8.

Byrne, P. (2000). Schizophrenia in the cinema: *Me, Myself and Irene. Psychiatric Bulletin, 24*(10), 364–365.

Corrigan, P. W., Watson, A. C., Gracia, G., Slopen, N., Rasinski, K., & Hall, L. L. (2005). Newspaper stories as measures of structural stigma. *Psychiatric Services, 56*(5), 551–556.

Daily Mail (2022). Off to the gym: The schizophrenic, 28, who used a screwdriver to kill an expectant mother the last time he was let out alone. https://www.dailymail.co.uk/news/article-10531125/Off-gym-schizophrenic-28-used-screwdriver-kill-expectant-mother.html

Diefenbach, D. L. (1997). The portrayal of mental illness on prime-time television. *Journal of Community Psychology, 25*(3), 289–302.

Fandom (2022). Criminal Minds Wiki: Schizophrenia. https://criminalminds.fandom.com/wiki/Schizophrenia

Greenstein, L. (2017). The best movies about mental health. National Alliance on Mental Illness. https://www.nami.org/Blogs/NAMI-Blog/December-2017/The-Best-Movies-About-Mental-Health

Gwarjanski, A. R., & Parrott, S. (2018). Schizophrenia in the news: The role of news frames in shaping online reader dialogue about mental illness. *Health Communication, 33*(8), 954–961.

Hoffner, C. A., & Cohen, E. L. (2018). A comedic entertainment portrayal of obsessive–compulsive disorder: Responses by individuals with anxiety disorders. *Stigma and Health, 3*(2), 159–169.

Lawson, A., & Fouts, G. (2004). Mental illness in Disney animated films. *The Canadian Journal of Psychiatry, 49*(5), 310–314.

Nairn, R. G., & Coverdale, J. H. (2005). People never see us living well: An appraisal of the personal stories about mental illness in a prospective print media sample. *Australian & New Zealand Journal of Psychiatry, 39*(4), 281–287.

Owen, P. R. (2012). Portrayals of schizophrenia by entertainment media: a content analysis of contemporary movies. *Psychiatric Services, 63*(7), 655–659.

Paramount (2022). Criminal Minds. https://www.paramountplus.com/shows/criminal_minds/

Parrott, S. (2020). Media stereotypes of mental illness: Nurturing and mitigating stigma. In A. C. Billings, & S. Parrott (Eds.), *Media stereotypes: From ageism to xenophobia* (pp. 239–257). Peter Lang.

Reuters (2015). Shyness, grieving soon to be classified as mental illness. *Fox News.* https://www.foxnews.com/health/shyness-grieving-soon-to-be-classified-as-mental-illness

Rosenstock, J. (2003). Beyond *A Beautiful Mind*: Film choices for teaching schizophrenia. *Academic Psychiatry, 27*(2), 117–122.

Signorielli, N. (1989). The stigma of mental illness on television. *Journal of Broadcasting & Electronic Media, 33*(3), 325–331.

The U.S. Sun (2022). Mind of a Monster: "I was driven to kill by 'the voice'". https://www.the-sun.com/news/4732460/kill-murder-the-voice-god-yorkshire-ripper-peter-sutcliffe/

Wilson, C., Nairn, R., Coverdale, J., & Panapa, A. (2000). How mental illness is portrayed in children's television: A prospective study. *The British Journal of Psychiatry, 176*(5), 440–443.

3

"Us" and "Them": Media & Stigma

In 2019, actor Joaquin Phoenix brought to life the legendary comic book character Joker, telling the arch villain's origin story on the big screen. The film won international prizes, including kudos from the prestigious Cannes Film Festival and 11 Academy Award nominations. It reached millions of viewers worldwide. It made history as the first R-rated movie to generate more than $1 billion in revenue (Desta, 2019).

The showing may have been helped, in part, by the film's controversy. Even before the film's release, critics condemned its storyline in which a lonely man with mental illness cannot find help and ultimately shoots a talk show host on live television after screaming "What do you get when you cross a mentally ill loner with a society that abandons him and treats him like trash?" It was only one murder in a week-long spree that saw the character smother his mother with a pillow, shoot three drunk men on the subway, and stab a colleague to death in a bloody rampage.

Critics described the movie as dangerous, claiming it would feed stereotypes that associate mental illness with violence. AMC, whose 950 locations make it the largest movie theater company in the world, agreed to show a 30-second public service announcement by the National Alliance on Mental Illness before each screening (Kroemer, 2019). In the PSA, a rotating cast of announcers describes a mystery illness you can catch by watching TV, listening to music, surfing the Internet, or even sitting in the movie theater. "What is this virus?" the announcers ask. "It's stigma." Contrasting this opposition, supporters called concerns over the film moral panic. Which side was correct? Might both claims be true, at least partially? Can movies and other mass media nurture stigma? We do not know for sure, but research suggests the mass media might feed stereotypes, prejudice, and discrimination related to mental illness.

Stereotypes

At the university library one recent afternoon, I searched for news articles about schizophrenia to see what journalists focused on when writing about the subject. The answer? Violence. Between 2000 and 2010, news reporters around the world associated violence and schizophrenia. A doctor diagnosed a notorious kidnapper with schizophrenia, one newspaper reported. In another paper, a woman with schizophrenia hanged herself in prison. In yet another, a medical team mistreated a man with schizophrenia who murdered his father.

Compare those results to 2011–2020 and a different picture emerges, one in which the overall narrative appears more promising and less focused on violence. One newspaper informed its readers of a study in which researchers sought to determine whether there was a link between marijuana use and schizophrenia. Another study suggests that owning a dog could help prevent schizophrenia. In another study, a poet described living with schizophrenia to a journalist, while a woman in England used art to maintain her mental health.

While modern news outlets are still publishing stigmatizing stories, newspapers, television shows, websites, and magazines are increasingly peppered with stories exploring the causes of mental disorders, describing novel treatments, and interviewing people who are affected by mental illness. The subtle change follows decades of stereotypical mass media content in which journalists and producers provided the public a narrow and extreme portrait of mental illnesses, both severe (e.g., schizophrenia) and common (e.g., depression).

At the same time, public attitudes toward mental illness appear to be changing. Ambivalent best describes public attitudes. In 2013, Angela M. Parcesepe and Leopoldo J. Cabassa reviewed 36 studies in which U.S. researchers gauged public attitudes toward mental illness. The U.S. public often endorsed a stereotypical association between violence and mental illness, they found, and this inaccurate belief lead people to want to avoid close social relationships with people who have a mental illness. Still, the U.S. public generally holds positive attitudes toward seeking professional treatment for mental illness, the researchers found. Support for coerced treatment, such as institutionalization and forced medication compliance, depended on the severity of a disorder and the perceived likelihood for violence.

Mixed attitudes also emerged in an international survey by Neil Seeman and colleagues (2016). The researchers surveyed 596,712 Web users from 229 countries to better understand public attitudes toward mental illness across cultures, political systems, and other differences. In *developed* countries such as the United States, 7% to 8% of respondents endorsed the statement that people with mental illness were more violent than others. In *developing* countries, the percentage reached 15% to 16%. Meanwhile, half of respondents in developed countries described mental illness as similar to physical illness, but 7% believed it could be overcome. The survey illustrates the complexity of public beliefs and attitudes about mental illness.

Attitudes concerning mental health, especially depression and anxiety, could improve following the COVID-19 pandemic. One in five U.S. adults told the Pew Research Center (Keeter, 2021) they experienced high levels of psychological distress during the pandemic, including sleeplessness, depression, anxiety, and loneliness. The survey found adults 18 to 29 were especially prone to distress, with 45% describing being "nervous, anxious or on edge."

Before the pandemic, another study (Horowitz & Graf, 2019) found that teenage boys and girls in the United States considered depression and anxiety a "major problem" among their peers. Indeed, the teens described anxiety and depression as bigger problems than bullying, poverty, teen pregnancy, gangs, and other issues. The concern cut across demographics, affecting teens from different races and economic backgrounds.

Altogether, there appear to be commonalities between the shifts in media content and public attitudes. The question arises, then: which influenced the other, the public or the media?

It's probably both.

The mass media mirror and inform society, shaping our perceptions of the world while also reflecting our values. Stories have used stereotypes about mental illness for dramatic effect since ancient Greece (at least), and the conflict between science and storytelling is just as old. In an interview with *The Atlantic*, William V. Harris, a professor of history at Columbia University, described how Greek physicians (in the 5th century B.C.) had to contest the idea that mental illness came from the gods (Beck, 2014). Mass storytelling is comparatively new, but television, radio, and print media carried on the tradition of employing mental illness to explain the unexplainable, demonize characters, or simply save time.

Researchers have used the idea of *priming* to explain how stereotypes might develop when a person reads a story, watches a show, or hears a song referencing depression, anxiety, suicide, or another term related to mental illness. Priming suggests that our minds operate as a network of connected concepts. The more often two concepts are prompted—or primed—at the same time, the closer they become in our minds. For example, if someone uttered the word "bread," the word "butter" would probably stand greater chance of coming to mind than "nurse" or "doctor." At the same time, the word "nurse" would probably elicit "doctor" faster than "butter" or "bread."

Through repetition, the association of violence/mental illness can become ingrained in our minds. To illustrate, imagine a college student sits down to read the news on his smartphone while eating breakfast. He sees a story headlined, "Accused murderer pleads not guilty by reason of insanity." He switches over to social media, where football fans are talking about the "insane" tackle doled out by an Alabama linebacker. It's the beginning of October, so he searches for scary Halloween costumes, thumbing past an advertisement in which a man wears a straightjacket covered in blood. Breakfast done, the student decides to play video games until class time, guiding his avatar through a digital world in which he must battle a mentally ill villain bent on world domination. Granted, it is unlikely a person would encounter stereotypes back-to-back while using mass media, but the story illustrates the dilemma: Stereotypes associating violence and mental illness abound, and the more we are exposed to such associations over time, the greater the likelihood we will call to mind the association while navigating the real world (Dillman Carpentier, 2017).

When we come upon a stimulus—a word such as bipolar, or a person who acts oddly—our minds quickly process the information and call to mind associations so we can act (or not). A person who watches a lot of crime TV should stand greater chance of calling to mind an association between violence and mental illness than someone who watches no TV, simply because the person's mind has been trained to associate violence and mental illness. An experiment by Ginny Chan and Philip T. Yanos (2018) illustrates the phenomenon. The researchers exposed 172 people to articles in which a violent event occurred. One article made reference to schizophrenia. Participants who encountered the reference—in other words, those who were primed—stood greater chance of subsequently blaming mental illness for the violence.

Of course, our individual experiences also shape how we think and act, probably more so than simple media exposure. We can also control our behavior (at times), so even when we immediately associate mental illness with violence, we can catch ourselves and act in a way that is not prejudicial. To illustrate, a student once complained to me about his roommate who had severe depression and anxiety. The roommate would not leave the dormitory or clean his room; he left dirty dishes lying around; he levied mean comments against the other roommates. For my student, the term "depression" would probably summon images of dirty dishes or verbal spats, because those real-world experiences trump any TV shows he watches.

Still, a portion of the American public may be under the impression they know no one affected by mental illness, or if they do, they may not have experienced so intimate a view as my student. In these cases, mass media content might plant false beliefs. For example, in Germany, researchers measured high school students' attitudes one week before and three weeks after they read newspaper articles associating mental illness and violent crime. The students were more likely to describe mentally ill people as violent and dangerous after reading the article (Dietrich et al., 2006).

Prejudice

Our beliefs—and stereotypes—are the seed for prejudice. Therefore, we are more likely to endorse negative attitudes toward people who experience mental illness when our minds summon associations such as "schizophrenia/violence" or "bipolar/dangerous." Toward this end, mass media exposure feeds prejudice by reinforcing negative emotions and beliefs concerning mental illness, or by implanting stereotypical beliefs. For example, Donald L. Diefenbach and Mark D. West (1997) examined how primetime television represented characters with mental illness, finding that these characters often perpetrated violence. In a second study, the researchers conducted a telephone survey of 419 U.S. adults, asking about their television viewing and attitudes concerning people with mental illness. They documented a relationship between viewing and prejudice—heavy television viewers considered the inclusion of mental health facilities in their neighborhoods as potentially dangerous for residents.

As illustrated in later chapters of this book, research suggests media exposure may also challenge prejudice. This potential informed the work of Nicole Mossing Caputo and Donna Rouner (2011), who had 137 university students engage with either a non-fiction or fictional narrative about a person with depression. Although the genre did not matter, the more students considered the story relevant, the more they identified with the main character. In turn, the more they identified with the character, the less distance they wished to maintain from people with mental illness.

A content analysis spearheaded by Anna Rae Gwarjanski reported comparable results in terms of the potential—good and bad—of media exposure on eliciting the expression of attitudes (Gwarjanski & Parrott, 2018). Gwarjanski examined news stories about schizophrenia that were drawn from traditional news organizations (e.g., *The New York Times*) and digital native websites (e.g., *Buzzfeed*). News organizations often covered schizophrenia in relation to violence—such as a mass shooting in Colorado—but journalists also peppered coverage with first-person narratives and articles about scientific and medical breakthroughs. In terms of attitudes, an analysis of reader comments showed that the stigmatizing articles elicited stigmatizing comments, apparently triggering anger, fear, and calls for coerced treatment of people with mental illness. The positive stories had a different result: Readers often shared their own experiences with mental illness or welcomed the scientific breakthroughs.

In addition to informing and illuminating attitudes, the mass media can normalize or challenge prejudice by providing evidence of social norms. Social norms are indicators of public opinion concerning beliefs, attitudes, or behaviors. People follow social norms to avoid being wrong; when you are unsure, you might assume others are behaving a certain way because they are in the know. In addition, people follow social norms to avoid social exclusion: One might face social sanctions for expressing ideas that are considered inappropriate.

The mass media shape social norms by communicating the commonality of attitudes and behavior, and also how other people will respond. For example, when Dallas Cowboys quarterback Dac Prescott publicly shared his experience with depression during the COVID-19 pandemic, a television commentator criticized Prescott's disclosure, saying it showed poor leadership and represented weakness. People swiftly condemned the statement on social media, and FoxSports, which carried the commentator's show, apologized. The initial comment illustrates an opinion vocalized by one person, stigmatizing depression. A person who only witnessed the commentary might reach the conclusion that disclosing mental illness to others is not a good idea. However, someone who also encountered the subsequent public condemnation could walk away with a different interpretation based on the social normative information conveyed.

Toward this end, research suggests comments beneath news stories, YouTube videos, and other mass media fare provide people information about social norms. For example, a recent study examined how comments beneath an offensive video shaped viewers' interpretations of the content. In the video, a popular comedian insulted an obese person. In one condition, comments condemned the humor as inappropriate. In the second condition, comments applauded the disparagement. People were more likely to report enjoying the video when it was accompanied by positive commentary. Presumably, viewers interpreted different norms being communicated and were hesitant to voice approval when they thought others were offended (Parrott, 2016).

The importance of social norms also informed a study in the wake of the 2020 presidential election in the United States (Parrott & Allen, 2021). The study compiled a list of the candidates from the 2016 and 2020 presidential elections, including Republican and Democratic primaries, and found instances in which the candidates used mental health-related language on Twitter and during formal debates. Overall, candidates did a poor job educating the public about the myriad issues facing mental health in the United States, including insurance parity, stigmatization, lack of funding for public systems, and mass incarceration of people with severe disorders. Instead, candidates used the massive platforms to use terms such as "crazy" and "insane" to insult one another. When the so-called leader of the free world calls others crazy on social media, and millions of followers like or share the comment, the event suggests such attitudes are common and socially supported.

Discrimination

Few researchers have actually studied mass media, mental illness, and discriminatory behavior. Instead, researchers often focus on people's intentions. Would they be willing to trust their children to a babysitter who has depression? Would they be willing to work alongside a person with schizophrenia? Often, after media exposure, the answer is "No."

Indeed, audiences consistently report increased desire to maintain social distance from people with mental illness after reading, watching, or otherwise consuming stereotypical media stories. For example, the Veterans & Media Lab at the University of Alabama examined readers' reactions to stereotypical news stories in which military veterans were associated with Post Traumatic Stress Disorder. Compared to people who did not read the stories, participants who encountered the media stereotypes subsequently produced higher estimates concerning the prevalence of PTSD among veterans. In turn, they reported greater desire to maintain social distance from veterans (Parrott et al., 2021).

In addition to social distance, researchers have found that stereotypes nurture discrimination in settings related to health care and government policy. In one study, heavy television viewers were more likely to consider a mental health facility in their neighborhood as a potential danger (Diefenbach & West, 1997). People perceive children with depression or ADHD as more likely to commit violence in school, and express willingness to use the legal system to force the children into treatment (Pescosolido et al., 2007). In one study (McGinty et al., 2013), researchers exposed readers to one of three news stories: a story about a mass shooting perpetuated by a mentally ill person; the same story accompanied by calls for restrictions on the sale of firearms to mentally ill people; or an article in which mental illness was not mentioned. The researchers wanted to know whether exposure to the articles would shape readers' attitudes toward people with mental illness and gun control laws, compared to a control group in which participants read no news story. In the end, participants who read the stories referencing mental illness stood greater likelihood of describing people with mental illness as violent and supporting measures to limit their access to firearms.

Researchers often use violent, visceral stereotypes when exposing research participants to mass media content about mental illness, including mass shootings and random acts of violence. Jonathan W.P. Bowman and Keon West (2019) wondered whether less obtrusive exposure might be equally problematic. The researchers exposed adults in the United Kingdom to Halloween costumes on the Internet while leading participants to believe they were helping with product research. One group of participants encountered a "Psycho Ward" costume that generated real-life controversy when it was sold by a grocery store chain. A control group saw different costumes. People who encountered the "Psycho Ward" costume subsequently reported more prejudice toward people with schizophrenia. Prejudice, in turn, led participants to anticipate negative social interactions with people diagnosed with schizophrenia.

In addition to public stigma, mass media content can elicit behavior that is detrimental toward oneself. For example, Cynthia Hoffner and colleagues (2015) surveyed American adults shortly after a gunman murdered 33 people at Virginia Polytechnic Institute and State University. People avoided activities that might reveal their own mental illness, presuming that extensive news coverage of the mass shooting had fed into negative attitudes toward people with mental illness.

Julia A. Maier and colleagues (2014) examined the relationships among mass media exposure, attitudes toward mental health professionals, perceptions of people seeking treatment, and self-stigma. The research team defined self-stigma as "negative feelings about oneself if one were to seek help for a mental health problem" (p. 251). The study determined that people's self-stigma was related to their attitudes about therapists and people who seek treatment. The media "are a powerful source shaping these perceptions," they concluded (p. 254).

Power

An argument can be made the mass media reinforce the status quo through the amplification of powerful voices—politicians, corporations—and the exclusion (or muffling) of minority voices. Screenwriters, reporters, and other content producers perpetuate stereotypes about mental illness because violence sells, critics contend. An article headlined "Schizo killer" will generate more clicks than an article headed, "Science reveals new treatment," and mental illness provides an easy explanation for unexplainable behavior in television shows and movies. In perpetuating myths, the mass media reinforce environments of power in which people with mental illness are marginalized, undervalued, and coerced.

Conclusion

The beginning of this chapter described the controversy surrounding the release of the film *Joker*, whose critics worried the film stigmatized mental illness. In the end, researchers confirmed the worry, at least in part. A team in New Zealand showed people the controversial film or another violent movie from the *Terminator* franchise that did not mention mental illness. Before airing the movie, the researchers gauged the audience's attitudes toward people with mental illness, including whether they deserve empathy, should be socially included, and would be violent. After the movie, the viewers were asked the same questions so researchers could compare before/after responses. While answers from *Terminator* viewers did not change, people's attitudes in the *Joker* camp changed—for the worse.

Still, the relationship between media and mental illness need not be negative. As the remainder of this book illustrates, a growing number of researchers are studying how media content might challenge stereotypes, prejudice, and discrimination. The following chapters illustrate this budding line of inquiry, illustrating how music, video games, celebrity testimonials, social media, and other mass media might mitigate the stigma attached to mental illness.

References

Bowman, J. W., & West, K. (2019). Prime and prejudice: Brief stereotypical media representations can increase prejudicial attitudes and behaviour towards people with schizophrenia. *Journal of Community & Applied Social Psychology, 29*(3), 167–177.

Chan, G., & Yanos, P. T. (2018). Media depictions and the priming of mental illness stigma. *Stigma and Health, 3*(3), 253.

Chung, J. E. (2019). Peer influence of online comments in newspapers: applying social norms and the social identification model of deindividuation effects (SIDE). *Social Science Computer Review, 37*(4), 551–567.

Desta, Y. (2019). Joker didn't just set a box office record this weekend. *Vanity Fair*. https://www.vanityfair.com/hollywood/2019/10/joker-box-office-opening-weekend-record

Diefenbach, D. L., & West, M. D. (2007). Television and attitudes toward mental health issues: Cultivation analysis and the third-person effect. *Journal of Community Psychology, 35*(2), 181–195.

Dietrich, S., Heider, D., Matschinger, H., & Angermeyer, M. C. (2006). Influence of newspaper reporting on adolescents' attitudes toward people with mental illness. *Social Psychiatry and Psychiatric Epidemiology, 41*(4), 318–322.

Dillman Carpentier, F. R. (2017). Priming. *The International Encyclopedia of Media Effects*, 1–14. Wiley.

Gwarjanski, A. R., & Parrott, S. (2018). Schizophrenia in the news: The role of news frames in shaping online reader dialogue about mental illness. *Health Communication, 33*(8), 954–961.

Hoffner, C. A., Fujioka, Y., Cohen, E. L., & Atwell Seate, A. (2017). Perceived media influence, mental illness, and responses to news coverage of a mass shooting. *Psychology of Popular Media Culture, 6*(2), 159.

Horowitz, J. M. & Graf, N. (2019). Most U.S. teens see anxiety and depression as a major problem among their peers. *Pew Research Center*. https://www.pewresearch.org/social-trends/2019/02/20/most-u-s-teens-see-anxiety-and-depression-as-a-major-problem-among-their-peers/

Keeter, S. (2021). Many Americans continue to experience mental health difficulties as pandemic enters second year. *Pew Research Center*. https://www.pewresearch.org/fact-tank/2021/03/16/many-americans-continue-to-experience-mental-health-difficulties-as-pandemic-enters-second-year/

Kroener, A. (2019). Mental health movie review. Joker is no joke! National Alliance on Mental Illness Cook County North Suburban. https://namiccns.org/2019/10/04/mental-health-movie-review-joker-is-no-joke/

Maier, J. A., Gentile, D. A., Vogel, D. L., & Kaplan, S. A. (2014). Media influences on self-stigma of seeking psychological services: The importance of media portrayals and person perception. *Psychology of Popular Media Culture, 3*(4), 239.

McGinty, E. E., Webster, D. W., & Barry, C. L. (2013). Effects of news media messages about mass shootings on attitudes toward persons with serious mental illness and public support for gun control policies. *American Journal of Psychiatry, 170*(5), 494–501.

Parcesepe, A. M., & Cabassa, L. J. (2013). Public stigma of mental illness in the United States: A systematic literature review. *Administration and Policy in Mental Health and Mental Health Services Research, 40*(5), 384–399.

Parrott, S. (2016). When everyone is laughing: The presence, characteristics, and enjoyment of disparagement humor in online TV. *Mass Communication and Society, 19*(1), 49–73.

Parrott, S., Albright, D. L., & Eckhart, N. (2021). Veterans and media: The effects of news exposure on thoughts, attitudes, and support of military veterans. *Armed Forces & Society*, 0095327X20986145.

Pescosolido, B. A., Fettes, D. L., Martin, J. K., Monahan, J., & McLeod, J. D. (2007). Perceived dangerousness of children with mental health problems and support for coerced treatment. *Psychiatric Services, 58*(5), 619–625.

Quintero Johnson, J. M., & Riles, J. (2018). "He acted like a crazy person": Exploring the influence of college students' recall of stereotypic media representations of mental illness. *Psychology of Popular Media Culture, 7*(2), 146.

Schomerus, G., Stolzenburg, S., Bauch, A., Speerforck, S., Janowitz, D., & Angermeyer, M. C. (2017). Shifting blame? Impact of reports of violence and mental illness in the context of terrorism on population attitudes towards persons with mental illness in Germany. *Psychiatry Research, 252*, 164–168.

Seeman, N., Tang, S., Brown, A. D., & Ing, A. (2016). World survey of mental illness stigma. *Journal of Affective Disorders, 190*, 115–121.

4

Where It Starts: Understanding the Creation of Media Content

When George Gerbner interviewed network censors in 1959 about mental illness on television, they deplored the use of terms such as "crazy" and "moron" and the association of mental illness with "comic, violent, or eerie situations" (p. 297). Gerbner noted that "These concerns arose partly out of personal involvement and conviction and partly under the pressure of viewer complaints and of professional and organizational activities in the mental health field."

By looking behind the curtain, Gerbner sought to understand the process of content creation, an area few researchers have explored in relation to mental illness in the decades since his study. As described in earlier chapters, our television shows, movies, news articles, and other mass media often perpetuate stereotypes about mental illness. A big question lingers, unanswered: Why?

Critics are quick to point to the almighty dollar. Shock, horror, and controversy are effective ways of capturing attention, and more eyes translate into more money through advertising, subscriptions, ticket sales, and downloads. It would be naive to discount the influential role of money in the creation of media content. However, it would be simplistic to dismiss media stereotypes as the product of financial ambitions alone. A number of factors shape the creation of our television shows, movies, and news stories. Writers, producers, directors and other content creators bring to the creative process personal attitudes, experiences, and motivations. The creators often work within the confines of organizations, such as production companies or newsrooms. Creators follow professional routines and guidelines, including deadlines, space limits, and time constraints. Other media professionals—such as public relations or advertising professionals—also shape the final product. Finally, content creators work within society and cultural norms, which can inform what is acceptable (or not), such as cursing, nudity, or the association of mental illness with "comic, violent, or eerie situations."

This chapter explores these factors, which provide the foundation for Pamela Shoemaker's work with gatekeeping theory and its hierarchy of influences (Shoemaker & Reese, 1996; Shoemaker & Vos, 2009). Research into the practices of mental health-related content creation remains scant. Still, Shoemaker's work highlights areas that researchers and mental health advocates should heed if they want to improve media representations of mental illness. These influences include characteristics of the individual content creator; their professional routines; the organization in which they work; the surrounding media ecosystem; and the social systems in which the media organization operates.

The Individual

When Gerbner interviewed TV censors, he came across an internal memo at one of the television networks. In the memo, an unnamed author described censors as spending more time advocating for mental health than arguably any other organization or institution in the United States. There could be many reasons behind the time commitment, the author wrote. The mental health association board included many members of the entertainment industry. More than your typical American, media professionals came into intimate contact with diverse segments of society. Finally, censors shouldered a "conscious moral responsibility" to audiences and "our own personal reaction to the great human tragedy" (p. 297).

The memo underscored the importance of the *individual* in the creation of media content, and the statement could be applied to movies, news stories, songs, and even social media posts concerning mental illness. Authors, directors, journalists, and other content creators bring personal experience and attitudes into the creative process. An individual's attitudes toward mental illness are important in shaping the stories told, viewpoints expressed, and lessons conveyed.

To illustrate, a journalist who understands stigma might hesitate to blame mental illness for a mass shooting. A screenwriter might avoid glamourizing suicide when she lost a personal friend to severe depression. A musician who suffers severe depression might use song lyrics to romanticize suicide. The way creators view mental illness matters, because their own thoughts and emotions inform the writing of songs, scripts, and news stories. Equally important are the attitudes creators hold toward subjects closely associated with mental health. For example, a writer who personally served in the Armed Forces might avoid representing all veterans as heroes or traumatized. Conversely, a pundit on the nightly news might deride a politician who took time off for mental health reasons. Anecdotes abound of sports commentators declaring professional athletes weak for taking time off for mental health (e.g., Bonesteel, 2020).

Journalists generally hold positive and liberal attitudes toward mental health and people with mental illness (Aoki et al., 2013). We lack studies concerning screenwriters' attitudes toward mental illness. Regardless, it would be daunting to change media representations of mental illness by adjusting individual attitudes given the sheer number of people involved in the creative process. For an illustration, simply watch the screen credits at the end of a movie or scroll through the homepage of a local news website. Dozens if not hundreds of people are involved in the creative process. Still, it can be attempted, and a growing number of advocacy organizations are working to boost knowledge and awareness among journalists, writers, and other creators. For example, mental health advocate and former first lady Rosalynn Carter founded Fellowships for Mental Health Journalism, which provide financial and professional support for journalists who are producing in-depth pieces related to mental health (Carter Center, 2022). Meanwhile, journalism organizations, universities, and mental health experts partnered on the Reporting Suicide project to help reporters produce informative yet sensitive stories about suicide. Journalists could walk away from the training with additional knowledge concerning the issue, plus tips on how they might improve their reporting routines (an influence on news content that is described in the next section).

Mental health advocates are also working to connect content creators and people with mental illness, because people who have lived experience can be sources for news stories, consultants on scripts, or even creators themselves. Toward this end, researchers are testing the potential for citizen journalism that "involves ordinary community members producing media pieces about topics and issues affecting them and their communities" (Carmichael et al., 2019). In Canada, Victoria Carmichael and her colleagues trained people with mental illness—schizophrenia, bipolar disorder, major depression—in the skills needed to become citizen journalists. Twice a week for two years, experts in videography, participatory video, journalism, and mental health trained the participants in scripting, videoing, and editing. The participants were asked to create videos about mental health, with complete control over the content. The sessions produced 26 videos, which the research team compared to randomly selected news stories produced by one of Canada's most popular television stations. The research team examined the videos for stigmatizing and counter-stigmatizing material, such as positive and negative tones, references to violence and crime, descriptions of poor treatment, stigma, and recovery. Compared to the professional news stories, pieces by citizen journalists were more likely to use positive tones and focus on recovery. Citizen journalists also were more likely to describe stigma as a problem facing people with severe mental illness. In contrast, the professional journalists were more likely to reference violence and crime. Further, professional journalists rarely interviewed people who had personally experienced mental illness.

Connecting journalists with sources is one way mental health advocates are attempting to help journalists improve coverage of mental illness. Journalists face numerous challenges when covering the subject, including generating story ideas, accessing sources, and finding time to produce in-depth pieces. In Australia, researcher Kate Holland (2018) interviewed nine health reporters about the role of journalists in covering mental health and the challenges they encounter. Holland (p. 1768) described the role of journalists "not as merely transmitters of the claims of medicine, science and public health, but as important mediators of the perspectives of actors within the health field who have a range of interests, agendas and media skills." Journalists acknowledged the role of personal experience in identifying subjects and issues to cover about mental health.

In the United States, Roma Subramanian (2014) interviewed 11 print journalists about how they identified, developed and wrote award-winning stories about mental health. In addition to personal experience with illness, professional experience informed the development and execution of news stories. Veteran reporters were able to apply skills to reporting and writing the stories. Their attitudes, helped, too (p. 818): "It appeared that a combination of respondents' empathy for their sources, non-stigmatizing attitudes toward mental illness, and understanding or knowledge of the illness facilitated good storytelling."

The studies highlight the importance of attitudes and personal experience in shaping the creation of mass media content. Still, journalists do not work in bubbles. Professional routines also shape mass media content. These include daily practices such as deadlines, space limitations, and ethical values.

The Routine

Imagine a journalist is working in a metro newsroom when a gunman murders four people downtown. Journalists are trained to answer specific questions (the "5Ws and H") when reporting on news events: who, what, when, where, why, and how. In this hypothetical scenario, police quickly provide answers for five questions, sharing the name of the man (who), the number of people injured (what), how they were injured, the time of day (when), and the location (where). Police cannot provide the reason the crime occurred because the investigation continues, but a detective shares that the gunman had been treated for depression. As the deadline looms, the journalist files his story, including reference to the shooter's mental health. Here, the values of time (a deadline), a newsworthy event (the shooting), and standard journalistic practices (answering the 5Ws and H) conclude by perpetuating a stereotype about mental illness.

A number of routines affect the work of people creating media content, including space considerations, deadline pressure, professional values, social networks, and goals. These factors might trump a journalist's individual attitudes concerning mental health, or a screenwriter's commitment to avoid stereotypes. For example, a friend who wrote situation comedies once told me about the time constraints facing scriptwriters. What is the quickest way to convey that a character is nerdy without a time-consuming backstory? Unfashionable eyeglasses. Time constraints might also explain the reason law-and-order television shows turn to mental illness to explain murderous behavior. A single word such as schizophrenia can quickly wrap up mysteries because it calls to mind (for some people) violence, and the home viewer often lacks actual understanding of the disorder to label the plotline unbelievable.

In the newsroom, journalists face time constraints while writing and reporting. Deadlines loom throughout the day during the 24-hour news cycle, limiting the amount of time journalists can interview sources, consult records, and meet people in the community. The deadline routine is probably one reason journalists consult elite sources when writing about mental health, interviewing medical professionals, researchers, and advocacy organizations instead of people who are actually affected by disorders. This is a problem, because readers or viewers are stripped of the opportunity to "meet" someone who is personally affected by mental illness. In addition, it limits the diversity of story ideas that journalists come up with. Australian journalists described their reliance on mental health organizations in connecting them with people who personally experienced mental illness (Holland, 2018). The results mirrored a finding by Subramanian (2014), who learned that U.S. journalists usually get their story ideas from sources who had personal experience with mental illness.

In addition to daily routines, journalists follow professional guidelines on how to report, write, photograph, and present stories. Journalists are trained to consider news values, or characteristics that render events, issues, and people newsworthy and interesting to mass audiences. Values include timeliness, proximity, conflict, and impact. Subramanian learned that U.S. journalists applied the values to an initial idea for a story before proceeding with reporting and writing. For example, one reporter described the values of novelty and surprise in prompting her award-winning coverage of mental health, saying she had initially encountered a statistic that more people in her state died by suicide than murder (Subramanian, 2014).

With insight into routines, advocates can help improve mass media content related to mental health. For example, the Reporting on Suicide foundation used its knowledge of journalism routines to identify best practices for the entire reporting process. The group advises reporters avoid sharing details about the method and specific location of a death. Reporters should avoid speculating about the dead person's motivations. They should provide data but avoid terms such as "epidemic" or "skyrocketing," because this could suggest suicide is common (and therefore acceptable).

Guidelines can be problematic despite the praise they generally receive from mental health advocates. Journalists told Holland (2018) that they balance the watchdog role of the press—where problems in the mental health system would be pointed out—with the desire to avoid harm by dampening public faith in the potential for treatment. Journalists also reported problems with advocacy organizations pushing too hard; rather than developing a working relationship, mental health advocates dictated demands to reporters. The approach backfired, leading journalists to avoid working with the organization. To illustrate, one journalist described numerous organizations all requesting their phone numbers be included at the bottom of stories about mental health.

Mental health advocates should recognize that journalists are not public relations practitioners or health communicators who are interested in advocating for a cause. Indeed, journalism schools teach budding reporters to present information to the public so they can make informed decisions for themselves. People have suggested news organizations balance out negative coverage by including more positive stories about mental health. This recommendation could backfire. As one reporter told Subramanian (2014, p. 820), journalists are not in the field of "propaganda" and should instead adopt a thoughtful approach to covering mental health that answers questions about underlying causes and consequences.

The Organization

Organizations—television networks, newspaper companies—can exert influence over media content. The political leaning of a news organization (e.g., Fox News versus MSNBC) can affect the way reporters frame subjects. For example, a conservative TV pundit might attribute a mass shooting to mental illness while a liberal commentator blames firearm access.

The motivations of the organization can also inform the creative process. For example, financial profit could drive a tabloid publication to share explicit details concerning the death by suicide of a beloved celebrity. Conversely, sense of community could lead a small town newspaper to feature a fundraiser on behalf of a halfway house for people with severe mental illness.

In the United States (and elsewhere), most people get their news from online sources such as news websites (e.g., CNN, Fox), aggregators such as Yahoo! and Google, and social media such as Facebook and Twitter. The transition toward digital news from newspapers and television drastically altered the business model of professional journalism, decimating news organizations' primary sources of income, advertising and subscriptions. News organizations now make money by tracking consumers' online behavior, cataloging which stories readers click, how long they spend with stories, and which stories receive "likes" and "shares" on social media. The information is used to guide editorial decisions (e.g., Vu, 2014). When it comes to mental health, Australian journalists told Holland (2018) that they seek out "case studies" in which a person can speak about living with mental illness. Case studies, or anecdotes, can illustrate the human side of illness. But there is a financial motive as well (p. 1774): "as one journalist observed they tend to be the stories that people share and linger on as evidenced by readership metrics."

An old journalism saying goes, "If it bleeds, it leads," meaning that stories of violence and death should be first on the evening news or front page because they capture public attention. As illustrated in Chapter 2, news organizations have developed a record of sensationalizing mental illness, mentioning mental illness in relation to crimes and violence. A study by Canadian researchers suggests journalists should instead favor positive stories if they wish to garner attention. Gavin Adamson and colleagues (2017) used Web analytics from three major Canadian publications to understand the types of stories readers were inclined to share with others. The result: People stood greater likelihood of sharing neutral stories about mental health and themes of recovery and intervention. A focus on violence and criminality did not increase the likelihood of a story being shared by readers. The research team writes that (p. 913), "The decades-old association that the news media make between mental illness and crime or violence is not amplified by the news audience. On the contrary, it is dampened, with readers preferring to share positive stories."

In addition to financial pressures, the structure of a news organization can influence its reporting on mental health. In the U.S., journalists underscored the importance of a supportive organizational environment in quality mental health reporting. Award-winning reporters described supportive editors who provided time and space for stories because they understood their importance, Subramanian reported (2014). These reporters spent weeks or months covering the stories, a perk that becomes less common as newsrooms downsize and the news cycle speeds up. The additional time afforded the journalists an opportunity to consult a wider breadth of sources. They also were able to consult public records and visit mental health facilities.

By understanding organizations, mental health activists can also better direct protests against offensive content. In 2017, the streaming service Netflix released a dramatic series called *13 Reasons Why*, in which a teenage protagonist dies by suicide. Before her death, the character leaves a collection of audio tapes for another teen to hear, sharing the reasons she killed herself. The show was controversial. Critics contended the storyline glamorized suicide and could be problematic for vulnerable viewers. Indeed, internet searches for "how to commit suicide" spiked after the release of the show, and suicide hotlines reported an increase in calls. People protested Netflix, which ultimately edited the storyline and affixed warning labels to episodes of the program. Ultimately the organization that funded and aired the program—not the writers or directors—controlled the message.

Social Institutional

The mass media operate within a web rather than a vacuum, one in which other media organizations can exert influence over the creative process. For example, *The New York Times* has been described as the newspaper of record, in part for its role in shaping the coverage of news organizations around the world. When its journalists deem a subject important enough to cover, other newsrooms might respond and assign reporters to the topic. Public relations and marketing can also help determine what gets told and how. For example, Netflix could remove a controversial comedian if it determines that the financial benefits are not worth the negative publicity.

Mental health advocates should understand the relationships among media outlets. How might the actions of one news organization, or one streaming service, inform the behavior of others? Does a chain own the local newspaper or television station? If so, a positive story could be picked up by sibling publications in the region or elsewhere in the nation. The landscape of news organizations has condensed. There were 672 major daily newspapers in the United States in April 2021, and seven companies owned more than half (Harvard, 2022). The largest was Gannett Co. Inc., which owned 250 daily papers. A story that runs in *The Tuscaloosa News*, a paper in Alabama, might be newsworthy enough to appear in *The Arizona Republic*, *Booneville Democrat* in Arkansas, the *Middletown Transcript* in Delaware, and the *Charlevoix Courier* in Michigan.

Social Systems

Finally, mass media operate within society, which means cultural values and norms can shape content. Social norms change over time. Partial nudity, violence, and profanity are common in network television programming, but cultural values suggest that such content only be shown after the children are (supposed to be) in bed. Social media afford audiences increased access to the actors, writers, and other creators, permitting them to condemn content they consider offensive while celebrating content deemed valuable.

In addition to cultural norms, journalists often operate under the guidance of professional norms. In the United States, for example, the Society for Professional Journalists provides an ethical code featuring guidelines for reporters, editors, and other news professionals. Among other recommendations, the guidelines encourage journalists to minimize harm when covering stories and to avoid sensationalism. Such themes emerged when researcher Anne O'Brien (2021) interviewed professional journalists in Ireland to understand their processes for reporting on mental health. Journalists described balancing their duty to inform the public with a desire to avoid harming people who are affected by mental illness and suicide. Journalists described sensitivity in language choice and detail. While avoiding harmful detail, journalists also described jargon—"died tragically" or "died suddenly" instead of "died by suicide"—as stigmatizing.

Conclusion

Mental health advocates can change media portrayals of mental illness when they understand how the writers behind the television, movie, computer, and smartphone screens operate. Advocates can protest television shows, movies, and news stories that stereotype mental illness. Readers can directly appeal to journalists, while individuals and organizations can develop educational resources to improve the professional routines of creators. When education falls short, advocates can threaten to deprive the mass media of audiences and, in turn, the dollar.

As one censor told Gerbner 70 years ago, people must appreciate the role of money in producing—and changing—mass media content. The censor offered a scenario: A producer spends big money making a show "which utilizes some poor, mentally disturbed soul as the villain terrorizing the countryside"(p. 302). The producer shops the show around, but one after another, stations reject the program, leaving the producer to "kiss fifty thousand bucks 'bye bye.'" The next time around, the censor said, "he will make darn sure his film is going to be acceptable before he starts producing it."

References

Adamson, G., Donaldson, L., & Whitley, R. (2017). Sharing recovery stories: Network gatekeeping of online news about mental illness. *Digital Journalism, 5*(7), 903–918.

Aoki, Y., Malcolm, E., Yamaguchi, S., Thornicroft, G., & Henderson, C. (2013). Mental illness among journalists: A systematic review. *International Journal of Social Psychiatry*, 59(4), 377–390.

Bonesteel, M. (2020). Skip Bayless condemned for saying Dak Prescott's admission of depression was a sign of weakness. *Washington Post.* https://www.washingtonpost.com/sports/2020/09/11/skip-bayless-dak-prescott-depression/

Carmichael, V., Adamson, G., Sitter, K. C., & Whitley, R. (2019). Media coverage of mental illness: A comparison of citizen journalism vs. professional journalism portrayals. *Journal of Mental Health, 28*(5), 520–526.

Carter Center (2022). The Rosalynn Carter Fellowships for Mental Health Journalism. https://www.cartercenter.org/health/mental_health/fellowships/

Gerbner, G. (1959). Mental illness on television: A study of censorship. *Journal of Broadcasting, 3*(4), 293–303.

Harvard University (2022). The future of media project. https://projects.iq.harvard.edu/futureofmedia/index-us-mainstream-media-ownership

Holland, K. (2018). Making mental health news: Australian journalists' views on news values, sources and reporting challenges. *Journalism Studies, 19*(12), 1767–1785.

Maiorano, A., Lasalvia, A., Sampogna, G., Pocai, B., Ruggeri, M., & Henderson, C. (2017). Reducing stigma in media professionals: Is there room for improvement? Results from a systematic review. *The Canadian Journal of Psychiatry, 62*(10), 702–715.

O'Brien, A. (2021). Reporting on mental health difficulties, mental illness and suicide: Journalists' accounts of the challenges. *Journalism, 22*(12), 3031–3047.

Reporting on Suicide (2022). Recommendations for Reporting on Suicide. https://reportingonsuicide.org

Shoemaker, P. J., & Reese, S. D. (1996). *Mediating the message* (pp. 781–795). Longman.

Shoemaker, P. J., & Vos, T. (2009). *Gatekeeping theory.* Routledge.

Subramanian, R. (2014). Covering mental illness: Challenges and solutions. *Journalism Practice, 8*(6), 809–825.

Vu, H. T. (2014). The online audience as gatekeeper: The influence of reader metrics on news editorial selection. *Journalism, 15*(8), 1094–1110.

5 Shaping the Agenda: Making Mental Health a "Top Issue"

Voters turned out in record numbers to decide who would become the 46th president of the United States, casting 158.4 million ballots in the 2020 General Election (Desilver, 2021). If the political spotlight could ever shine on mental health policy, this would have been the year. The nation (and world) found itself in the COVID-19 pandemic, which killed millions of people and devastated families. Unemployment reached its highest rates since the end of World War II (Falk et al., 2021), creating financial stress for many Americans. People experienced isolation as they maintained social distance to avoid spreading illness, becoming deprived of direct contact with friends and family. Americans, especially African Americans, experienced anger, fear, and stress after seeing unarmed people shot or choked to death by police (Bor et al., 2018; Pazzanese, 2021). The confluence of events created ever-steady emotional turmoil, a recipe for depression, anxiety, and other issues.

In the run-up to the election, millions of people turned to television and social media for debates in which contenders to be "Leader of the Free World" discussed how they would handle pressing issues facing the country, including the growing number of people experiencing depression, anxiety, and other mental health issues. Instead, viewers saw Donald Trump, the Republican incumbent, describe gun-free zones as "target practice" for "sickos" and "the mentally ill" (Parrott & Allen, 2021). They saw Bernie Sanders, a Democratic contender, tell an audience in Flint, Michigan, that they should simply look at Republicans if they wanted to understand why the nation needs better mental health care. They saw candidates use social media to describe opponents as "batshit crazy," "crazies," "losing their minds," "nutjobs," "nuts," "unhinged," "wacko," and "basketcase." Candidates spent more time levying insults in debates and social media than discussing funding for mental health, stigma, health insurance parity, or other relevant subjects (Parrott & Allen, 2021). If U.S. voters were looking for politicians to talk about mental health, they were out of luck.

Politicians, news outlets, and other elites help set the agenda for public dialogue related to social issues, politics, health, and other subjects (Coleman et al., 2009). There is a famous saying in mass media research: The media do not tell the public *what to think*, but *what to think about*. The idea is called agenda setting, and it has inspired hundreds of research studies in mass communication, political science, sociology and other fields since the 1970s (McCombs, 2005). Coleman and colleagues (2009, p. 147) defined it as "the process of the mass media presenting certain issues frequently and prominently with the result that large segments of the public come to perceive those issues as more important than others." In newsrooms around the world, journalists must sift through millions of daily life occurrences to determine which events warrant news coverage. In doing so, journalists can increase the amount of attention the public affords a subject such as mental health. Conversely, journalists can remove an issue from the agenda for public discussion. Of course, the process is complicated because journalists do not work within vacuums: elite sources, such as politicians, can also influence public opinion, and the rise of social media has afforded the public a prominent seat at the table.

Donald Shaw and Max McCombs, two researchers at the University of North Carolina, are credited with developing and popularizing agenda setting at a time when the public got its news from a few sources, such as local television, community newspapers, *The New York Times*, and magazines such as *Newsweek*. In a seminal study, Shaw and McCombs discovered that the more coverage news outlets devoted to a particular subject—say mental health policy—the more the voting public considered it an important issue (McCombs & Shaw, 1972).

Journalists increase the salience, or the perceived importance, of issues by declaring items newsworthy and sharing information in headlines, photographs, print stories, and video. For example, on Valentine's Day 2022, the U.S. House Committee on Energy & Commerce held a hearing on "Americans in Need: Responding to the National Mental Health Crisis." Members of Congress discussed mental health challenges from the COVID-19 pandemic, hearing testimony from mental health advocates, researchers, and medical professionals. A confluence of factors prompted lawmakers to spend time discussing depression, anxiety, suicide, and personal loss during the pandemic, including news coverage. The United States witnessed a spike in the number of news stories about mental health during the pandemic. NewsBank data shows 230,600 U.S. newspaper stories referenced mental health in 2019. The number increased to 275,166 in 2020.

As noted in Chapter 4, journalists also respond to the coverage of other news outlets. If an influential publication such as *The New York Times* deems a subject newsworthy, journalists for other news outlets might respond with stories of their own, a phenomenon called intermedia agenda setting (Coleman et al., 2009). The dominos may continue to fall until an issue provides fodder for the commentators on cable news networks, social media, and radio. In addition, a small contingent of corporations own the majority of daily newspapers in the United States, sharing content among sibling publications. A reporter in one newsroom could write about the importance of children's mental health, and the story could appear the next day in dozens more newspapers around the country.

Researchers originally focused their attention on the relationship between the news media and public agendas. In other words, how does the news media's attention shape which issues the public thinks are important? Researchers have also described a policy agenda, or the issues considered important by lawmakers, government health officials, and other people in decision-making roles.

Agenda Setting and Mental Health: Existing Research

Compared to physical health, mental health has often been overlooked by the government, policy makers, insurance companies, and the general public. In the influential *New England Journal of Medicine*, Anne E. Becker and Arthur Kleinman (2013, p. 66) wrote that "this historical divide – in practice and in policy – between physical health and mental health has in turn perpetuated large gaps in resources across economic, social, and scientific domains. The upshot is global tragedy: a legacy of the neglect and marginalization of mental health."

Agenda setting is an indirect approach by which advocates might change attitudes, behavior, and policy related to mental health. Advocates can identify problems facing mental health, advocate novel solutions, and solicit change through mass media attention rather than, say, directly appealing to lawmakers. Mass communication researchers have paid little attention to the subject of agenda setting in relation to mental health. Still, researchers in fields such as public health have used the theory to inform studies concerning news media, public agendas, and policy agendas.

To illustrate, Sharon Beder, Richard Gosden, and Loren Mosher (2003) argued that pharmaceutical companies in the United States and Australia employed sophisticated public relations campaigns to direct the agenda for public dialogue and policy regarding mental health. The authors questioned the motivations of the companies, describing their intentions as profit-driven, and warned against the outcome for mental health consumers and society at large. Beder and colleagues describe the growth of "policy-entrepreneurs who build up advocacy coalitions to push policies onto the agenda" (p. 1), a growing area of agenda setting in which public relations plays an important role. Pharmaceutical companies use "front groups" to push policy and shape public debate "behind a cover of community concern" (p. 2), because "it is far more effective to have a group of citizens or a group of experts — preferably a coalition of such groups — which can publicly promote the outcomes desired by the corporation whilst claiming to represent the public interest" (p. 2).

Australia and the United States witnessed the triumph of the biological explanation for mental illness—and medication as treatment—over therapy because of such agenda setting, the authors argue (Beder et al., 2003). Pharmaceutical companies used a three-prong approach to setting the mental health agenda in each country, the authors contend, using advocacy groups to simulate public interest; planting stories in the media to generate public support for policies; and hiring lobbyists to directly reach lawmakers. "The cynical way in which this shaping, packaging and selling has been carried out in regard to mental health policy-making over the last couple of decades should serve as a warning to anyone who believes that the public good should come before corporate profits," the authors write (p. 10).

Nicole Votruba and colleagues (2020, p. 426) define *policy agenda setting* as "the pre-decision process when a problem is identified, defined and prioritized, gains and maintains attention of policymakers, and eventually becomes a policy priority." The policy agenda is clearly important for advocates who are interested in growing legislative attention for mental health. Votruba and colleagues proposed a model for mental health-related policy agenda setting in low- and middle-income countries. The model moves well beyond the McCombs and Shaw theory of agenda setting, incorporating different actors (e.g., doctors, media, religious leaders), evidence generators (e.g., research, science outreach), political contexts, and other influences to explain how an item might be placed upon the policy agenda.

Indeed, the number of players involved in setting public and policy agendas increased since the days of the seminal McCombs and Shaw study. Harvey A. Whiteford and colleagues (2016) illustrated how the confluence of news coverage, advocacy, politics and simple luck can inform a national agenda for mental health policy. In Australia, a team led by Whiteford investigated how youth mental health appeared on the nation's agenda in 2011, leading the government to invest hundreds of millions of dollars in two youth mental health programs. The researchers examined numerous records, including transcripts from parliamentary proceedings, committee meetings, research publications, and news reports, to understand how interest in youth mental health changed over time. Five major elements ultimately thrust youth mental health on the policy agenda. First, advocates, health experts, and news outlets identified problems facing the mental health of the nation's youth. Second, the two programs stood at the ready for implementation; they were well-advertised and pre-tested. Third, political turmoil provided an opportunity for an opposition party that featured youth mental health among its policies. Fourth, high-profile "policy entrepreneurs," or mental health advocates, used the mass media to criticize politicians for maintaining the status quo in relation to mental health. Fifth, the time was opportune: the government was preparing its annual budget.

The nation's news media played an important role throughout the agenda-setting process, illustrating problems facing youth (such as suicide), and amplifying criticism of political leaders. The researchers also noted the significant role of the "media-savvy" public. "Public pressure . . . did not necessarily reflect the views of a representative section of the voting public," they concluded (p. 8). "Rather, it was a group that could be termed 'the conspicuous public,' those who most effectively utilized social media to make their views known, and thus became important influences of agenda setting on this issue."

The Australian case demonstrates strategies described by Charles T. Kozel and colleagues (2006), who underscored the importance of agenda setting in health promotion and provided recommendations for health advocates to ensure issues are elevated (and kept) on the media, public, and policy agendas. Kozel and colleagues recommended mental health advocates develop relationships with media professionals, such as journalists, and illustrate how an issue such as mental health represents a shared problem for different segments of society. Once an issue becomes prominent on the media, public and policy agendas, advocates should also work to ensure it remains salient.

Social Media and the Rise of Other Influencers

A limited section of society once enjoyed the power to shape the public and policy agendas. Journalists chose which subjects to cover and how (e.g., a big headline on the front page, or tiny blurb tucked away on Page 12A). Politicians introduced bills (prompting news coverage), manufactured controversy (generating debate), and deemed issues important (eliciting attention). Everything changes, though, and the widespread adoption of social media in the early 2000s empowered audiences to shape which issues the public, news media, and politicians consider important. The shift is incredibly important for mental health advocates.

Indeed, researchers in Australia (Dadich & Khan, 2021) studied how three mental health organizations established the agenda for youth dialogue about mental health on the social media platform Twitter. Ann Dadich and Aila Khan at Western Sydney University (2021) sought to determine how youth mental health appeared on the public agenda in Australia, where depression and anxiety are common among teens. The researchers drew 14,698 tweets that referenced 3 youth-focused mental health organizations in Australia, and then culled the tweets to 600 (200 for each organization). The researchers then examined the remaining tweets to determine, as McCombs and Shaw described, how the posts illustrated "what to think about."

When people referenced the organizations on Twitter, they often did so in a positive way, sharing resources offered by the organizations or responding in a positive tone to the organization itself. Users also shared research related to mental health. The information shared by users reflected each organization's focus; for example, the ReachOut organization offers online support for youth, and Twitter comments reflected the mission. Mental health practitioners, the authors concluded, should mind the key lesson that "social media, like Twitter, can be strategically used to situate their agenda within public discourse" (p. 245). Another interesting conclusion involved the relationship among the three organizations in the study: The organizations shared each other's information via Twitter, essentially offering each other support toward the mission of youth mental health, and in doing so they demonstrated what mass communication researchers call intra-media agenda setting.

Social media has also afforded mental health advocates the opportunity to shape the public agenda without including journalists as a middleman. An increasing number of celebrities are using social media to share stories of personal experience with mental health issues. Celebrities often reach more people than traditional news outlets. *The New York Times*, one of the world's most influential news sources, has 51 million followers on Twitter. Demi Lovato, a singer and mental health advocate, has 54 million. When influential celebrities describe mental health as a pressing problem, their comments can inform the public and policy agendas. For example, the four-episode documentary "Dancing with the Devil" discussed Lovato's career and personal life, including a near-fatal drug overdose in 2018. In addition to its own audience, the documentary generated dozens of news stories about the popular singer and mental health.

Factors Affecting Agenda Setting

A number of factors intervene in the relationship between the news media, public, and policy agendas. Renita Coleman and colleagues (2009) describe two factors as particularly important: need for orientation and obtrusiveness. Need for orientation is defined as "a psychological concept that describes individual differences among people in their desire to understand a new environment or situation by turning to the media" (p. 152). It peaks when a person experiences high uncertainty and high relevance. In other words, a person should experience need for orientation when they are interested in a subject (relevance) but clearly do not know enough to make informed decisions (uncertainty). In such instances, the person should become more dependent upon the news in determining which issues are important.

Obtrusiveness is "when people have direct, personal experience with an issue" (p. 152). People are less dependent on the news for information about issues they have already experienced. The COVID-19 pandemic rendered depression and anxiety more obtrusive for many people. Depression became more common (Ettman et al., 2020). The mantra long sounded by mental health advocates—"it can happen to anyone"—sunk in for people who doubted or ignored the message.

Second-Level Agenda Setting

Researchers have identified a second level to agenda setting in which researchers abandon the original motto and agree that the media do indeed tell people *what to think*. This second-level agenda setting describes how the news media (a) increase the salience of issues for the public while also (b) communicating how people should think about the issues. For example, Republican candidates in the 2020 presidential election blamed mass shootings on mental illness, while

Democratic candidates attributed firearm access as the culprit. Mass shootings emerged on the agenda because of extensive news coverage, and by covering the candidates, the media attributed the crimes to different causes.

As illustrated in Chapter 2, this second-level of agenda setting can be problematic given the mass media's track record of perpetuating stereotypes about mental illness. The mass media often frame mental disorders as the impetus for violent behavior. Still, it appears that journalists might be shifting the narrative. They are interviewing people who actually experience mental illness, which humanizes the condition. They are writing about scientific breakthroughs, including advances in treatment and prevention. They are sharing stories of protest, in which people directly challenge stereotypical thinking about mental illness.

The shift may be due in part to a new generation of journalists entering the newsroom and bringing with them more positive attitudes toward mental health. A number of training programs and guidelines are being offered by universities, mental health groups, and others to help journalists understand how news coverage can be problematic or helpful (e.g., Reporting on Suicide, 2021). While journalists are trained to avoid sharing their own opinions, they do embrace professional values of minimizing harm and avoiding stereotypes.

Mental health, then, is garnering increased attention as an important issue (agenda setting), and the messages being communicated are becoming increasingly positive (second-level agenda setting, or framing).

Conclusion

The role of the traditional news media remains important in shaping the public agenda related to mental health. Still, mental health advocates must also consider the role of other forces in shaping the public agenda, including social media and elite sources such as politicians.

Agenda setting remains relevant for numerous reasons. First, news coverage legitimizes subject matter. National news coverage can communicate to audiences that yes, they should be paying attention to the latest topic trending on social media. Second, the relationship among elites, journalists, and social media resembles a loop rather than one-way road. For example, a presidential candidate might generate news coverage by making an offhand comment about mental health, bringing public attention to the subject in a controversial way. Finally, news outlets still reach millions (if not billions) of people. They remain influential, even if people have alternative ways to gather information about events, issues, and people.

Despite their dire description of the world's historical marginalization of mental health, compared to physical health, Becker and Kleinman (p. 71) concluded that "Mental health has arrived on the global health agenda; establishing it as a priority at the highest level is essential to match aspiration to need."

References

Becker, A. E., & Kleinman, A. (2013). Mental health and the global agenda. *New England Journal of Medicine, 369*(1), 66–73.

Beder, S., Gosden, R., & Mosher, L. (2004). Pig Pharma: Psychiatric agenda setting by drug companies. In *Family therapy as an alternative to medication* (pp. 196–213). Routledge.

Bor, J., Venkataramani, A. S., Williams, D. R., & Tsai, A. C. (2018). Police killings and their spillover effects on the mental health of black Americans: A population-based, quasi-experimental study. *The Lancet, 392*(10144), 302–310.

Coleman, R., McCombs, M., Shaw, D., & Weaver, D. (2009). Agenda setting. In *The handbook of journalism studies* (pp. 167–180). Routledge.

Dadich, A., & Khan, A. (2021). Using Twitter to promote a youth mental health agenda. *Health Promotion International, 36*(1), 235–249.

DeSilver, D. (2021). Turnout soared in 2020 as nearly two-thirds of eligible U.S. voters cast ballots for president. *Pew Research Center.* https://www.pewresearch.org/fact-tank/2021/01/28/turnout-soared-in-2020-as-nearly-two-thirds-of-eligible-u-s-voters-cast-ballots-for-president/

eSafety (2021). The digital lives of Aussie teens. *eSafety Commissioner, Australian Government.* https://www.esafety.gov.au/sites/default/files/2021-02/The%20digital%20lives%20of%20Aussie%20teens.pdf

Ettman, C. K., Abdalla, S. M., Cohen, G. H., Sampson, L., Vivier, P. M., & Galea, S. (2020). Prevalence of depression symptoms in US adults before and during the COVID-19 pandemic. *JAMA Network Open, 3*(9), e2019686–e2019686.

Falk, G., Romero, P. D., Nicchitta, I. A., & Nyhof, E. (2021). Unemployment rates during the COVID-19 pandemic. *Congressional Research Service.* https://sgp.fas.org/crs/misc/R46554.pdf

Kozel, C. T., Kane, W. M., Hatcher, M. T., Hubbell, A. P., Dearing, J. W., Forster-Cox, S., . . . & Goodman, M. (2006). Introducing health promotion agenda-setting for health education practitioners. *Californian Journal of Health Promotion, 4*(1), 32–40.

McCombs, M. (2005). A look at agenda-setting: Past, present and future. *Journalism Studies, 6*(4), 543–557.

McCombs, M. E., & Shaw, D. L. (1972). The agenda-setting function of mass media. *Public Opinion Quarterly, 36*(2), 176–187.

Parrott, S., Billings, A. C., Hakim, S. D., & Gentile, P. (2020). From# endthestigma to# realman: Stigma-challenging social media responses to NBA players' mental health disclosures. *Communication Reports, 33*(3), 148–160.

Parrott, S., & Allen, H. G. (2021). Swapping insults, neglecting policy: How US Presidential candidates communicate about mental health. *Health Communication*, 1–9. DOI: 10.1080/10410236.2021.1980252.

Pazzanese, C. (2021). How unjust police killings damage the mental health of Black Americans. *The Harvard Gazette.* https://news.harvard.edu/gazette/story/2021/05/how-unjust-police-killings-damage-the-mental-health-of-black-americans/

Reporting on Suicide (2021). Recommendations for reporting on suicide. https://reportingonsuicide.org

Votruba, N., Grant, J., & Thornicroft, G. (2020). The EVITA framework for evidence-based mental health policy agenda setting in low-and middle-income countries. *Health Policy and Planning, 35*(4), 424–439.

Wallack, L., & Dorfman, L. (1996). Media advocacy: A strategy for advancing policy and promoting health. *Health Education Quarterly, 23*(3), 293–317.

Whiteford, H. A., Meurk, C., Carstensen, G., Hall, W., Hill, P., & Head, B. W. (2016). How did youth mental health make it onto Australia's 2011 federal policy agenda? Sage Open, *6*(4), 2158244016680855.

6

The Power of Celebrity: How Our Identification with Media Characters and Personalities Can Combat Stigma

The legendary American swimmer Michael Phelps once produced a documentary about mental health called *The Weight of Gold,* sharing the stories of elite athletes who experienced depression, anxiety, suicidal thoughts, and other mental health issues while they trained and competed in the Olympic games. One by one, athletes described how competing in the Olympics cultivated stress in romantic relationships, friendships, employment, self-esteem, and other areas of life. One by one, they described a cultural environment in which athletes are told to suck it up, tough it out, keep pushing. Phelps, the most decorated Olympian of all time, spearheaded the film because the stories resonated with him. Phelps said he spent so long focusing on swimming that he neglected other areas of life, and beyond the pool he plummeted into depression and suicidal ruminations.

The story might be unexpected from a man who broke world records, won 28 medals, and made millions through endorsement deals. That is one reason the story—and the experiences of other Olympians—resounded with home audiences. *The Weight of Gold* attracted millions of viewers and critical recognition, but its greatest accomplishment came through the public dialogue it generated. People talked about the documentary at work. They attended panels in which Olympians spoke about mental health. They read news articles and celebratory reviews of the documentary, commented on social media, and shared the movie trailer with friends. They even talked about their own experience with mental illness, inspired by the disclosures from athletes who had reached the pinnacle of competition.

In an interview, Phelps told me that the responses to his own disclosure have "been absolutely incredible hearing. It's almost like it's giving people a voice. I think that's the most powerful thing."

The documentary is only one example of celebrities pulling back the curtain on their personal lives and sharing their own stories of living with depression, anxiety, and other mental health issues. We are witnessing a sea change in public conversations about mental health, led by a growing number of athletes, musicians, writers, actors, and other celebrities whose personal stories encourage others to seek help and challenge stigma. The list of celebrities who recently disclosed experience with depression, anxiety, negative moods, or other issues includes singers (Demi Lovato, Rihanna), basketball stars (Kevin Love, DeMar DeRozan), race car drivers (Lewis Hamilton, Lando Norris), rappers (Kendrick Lamar, Kid Cudi), professional football players (Brandon Marshall, Calvin Ridley), and actors (Chris Evans, Jim Carey). Indeed, *Harper's Bazaar* published a compilation of "39 celebrities who have opened up about mental health," presenting the story as "Proof that anxiety and depression can affect anyone" (Roberts, 2018, para. 1).

Celebrity disclosures can help mitigate public stigma by challenging traditional notions concerning mental illness, normalizing open conversation, and inspiring people to disclose mental illness and/or seek treatment. Celebrity disclosures can also be empowering for the person who shares. People who disclose might feel relief and empowerment, as well as reduced stress when compared to being "in the closet" and fearing a day when people discover their secret. A spur-of-the-moment decision led Phelps to disclose his experience with depression to a *Sports Illustrated* reporter, and Phelps described the interview as a life-changing moment. "When something is holding you back for so long, and then you just drop it and keep walking . . . that's what I felt like," he said. "'This is awesome. That's how easy it is.'"

This chapter illustrates examples in which celebrities publicly shared personal experience with mental illness, an important moment in destigmatizing mental illness. Scholarship into the subject is limited, but researchers are interested in several questions related to celebrity disclosures. First, researchers are interested in the reason celebrities share, and how they use mass media to do so. Second, scholars are interested in the actual content of the disclosures. What do celebrities share? Third, researchers want to understand how audiences respond to the disclosures. As described below, a budding line of research suggests celebrity disclosures positively affect beliefs, attitudes, emotions, and behavioral intentions.

Motivations for Celebrity Disclosures

A spur-of-the-moment decision led Phelps to tell a trusted reporter about his experiences with depression and suicidal thoughts. Naomi Osaka, the Japanese tennis champion, informed fans of her depression and anxiety after feeling pressured by international tennis officials and French Open organizers. DeMar DeRozan, the basketball star, shared a tweet that was ambiguous because it directly quoted song lyrics: "This depression get the best of me." In 2020, I began working alongside my colleague Andrew C. Billings, an internationally renowned sports media scholar, to better understand the reason elite athletes use mass media to disclose mental illness. We interviewed athletes from diverse sports (rugby, football, swimming) and backgrounds (race, gender, nationality). Despite their diverse backgrounds and illnesses, we noticed four common motivations behind the disclosures. The first motivation could be classified as *personal fulfillment*. Second, athletes were inspired by the example of fellow athletes and mental health advocates, a theme we refer to as *inspiration*. Third, athletes embraced their position as *role models* in society, recognizing their disclosures could educate the general public while encouraging people to seek help, challenge stigma, and openly talk about mental health. Fourth, athletes faced circumstances in which they felt compelled to disclose, a *protective* approach.

The timing of the disclosures helps provide additional context. Several athletes came forward during the COVID-19 pandemic, a period that reinforced the fact mental illness can affect anyone. People struggled through unemployment, social isolation, disconnection from family and friends, serious illness, and death. In 2020, the sporting world closed—games were canceled, seasons shelved, and the Summer Games postponed—and professional athletes found themselves without the ability to compete. The loss of competition proved especially problematic for athletes whose identities were rooted in work, a common occurrence in professional sport where success means constantly working out, practicing, and competing. In a documentary on Netflix, three-time Grand Slam champion Naomi Osaka questioned her identity outside tennis, asking "Who am I if I am not good at tennis?" Kevin Love, the NBA star, pondered a comparable question when the pandemic suddenly halted the basketball season. In an essay for *The Player's Tribune*, Love recounted wondering, "Who am I outside basketball?"

The comments by Love and Osaka hint at one reason celebrities disclose experience with mental illness. Mental illness can become important parts of people's *identities*, especially long-lasting conditions, and keeping mum about a condition can leave a person feeling as though they are not being their true selves. Celebrities are personas, which means there are essentially two people wrapped up in one: the real human, and then the persona that fans *think* they know. As Love recounted, there was Kevin Love the basketball player, and then Kevin Love the person. In his *Player's Tribune* essay, Love describes the first moment he walked into a room as the real Kevin Love as joyous. "One of the best days of my life happened after I started working through my issues with a therapist, and I walked into a room for the first time, and I was just 100% my authentic self," Love wrote (2020, para. 41). Similarly, Michael Phelps recounts shedding his "Golden Child Olympian" image for the "real me" and adopting an attitude that if others don't like it, well, too bad. In her memoir (2012), the four-time Olympic swimmer Amanda Beard describes the conflict between her identity and the squeaky-clean image cultivated by the news media. Beard disclosed her experience with depression, obsessive compulsive tendencies, self-harm, and body dysmorphia in her memoir *In the Water They Can't See You Cry*. She wrote, "People easily forget that athletes are human and not a public commodity to be tossed aside when the dividends on everyone's emotional investment are disappointing" (p. 119). Even though she hesitated at first, she says disclosing the truth about her personal life proved empowering.

In addition to personal fulfillment, celebrities disclose mental illness after being inspired by the example of others. DeRozan hinted at his mental health through a tweet quoting musician Kevin Gates, who rapped about depression. Love, another All-Star basketball player, subsequently cited DeRozan's disclosure as an impetus for his disclosure of anxiety and depression. Osaka informed French Open officials she would not do press conferences during the 2021 tournament to protect her mental health, receiving backlash from tennis officials and fellow players. She spoke to Michael Phelps, who told her that sharing her story of depression and anxiety might save someone else's life. If that was the case, she said, it would be worth it.

The basketball player Charles Barkley once famously said "I am not a role model." While the sentiment is applaudable, the opposite is true. Celebrities are role models, for better or worse, and many celebrities understand how their own stories could inspire others to seek help when it comes to mental illness. The model Chrissy Teigen shared her experience with post- partum depression after the birth of her daughter, Luna. "I'm speaking up now because I want people to know it can happen to anybody and I don't want people who have it to feel embarrassed or to feel alone" (Singh, 2020, para. 8). Beard decided she would publicly share her mental health journey after a trusted reporter for *The New York Times* suggested it would help other young women who went through comparable struggles.

Finally, celebrities may feel compelled to publicly disclose mental illness because of external pressure. Simone Biles, the world-renowned gymnast, withdrew from competition during the 2020 Olympics because she experienced the twisties, a gymnastics term for mental/physical imbalance. Her withdrawal from looming competition shone a megawatt spotlight on the question "Why?" which she ultimately explained as mental health related. People accused Osaka of abusing the word "mental health" when she explained her reasoning for avoiding press conferences at the French Open, so Osaka eventually withdrew from competition and shared that she had been experiencing depression and anxiety for years. In an essay in *Time* magazine, headlined "It's OK not to be OK," the Japanese superstar explained that she hoped she would never feel compelled to speak about her medical history again.

How—and What—Celebrities Disclose

When the time came for Phelps to disclose, he chose a trusted journalist.

Osaka used Instagram.

The actress Carrie Fisher broadcast her experience with bipolar disorder, sharing details in news interviews, public service announcements, and a memoir.

Celebrities have used several methods for sharing their stories about mental health, including mainstream media, social media, and advocacy work. Each method has pros and cons for the celebrity. Mainstream media—such as news interviews—permit celebrities to reach diverse and large audiences. However, journalists control the gates of information, meaning celebrities can be forced to relinquish control over their personal narrative. Social media affords celebrities the chance to bypass the traditional gatekeepers and speak directly to followers. It provides the chance for dialogue, permitting fans to post comments and offer validation to the celebrity. Still, dialogue is a double-edged sword. Social media can quickly become toxic, so disclosures can elicit verbal abuse.

Celebrities (and other people) face decisions concerning when, how, and what to share when disclosing personal experience with mental illness. Some celebrities have used the mass media to disclose general information about their mental health. For example, Osaka used Instagram to inform fans she experienced depression and anxiety, without providing details concerning symptoms, treatment, and other experiences. Other celebrities adopt the approach of "broadcasting" their conditions. Broadcasting is a form of disclosure in which an individual shares a stigmatized condition while also taking pride in their identity (Corrigan & Rao, 2012). Demi Lovato has detailed her experiences with bulimia and other conditions, sharing photographs and personal stories about the role of mental illness in her life. She also served as an executive producer for a documentary called "Beyond Silence," in which three people discuss how speaking up about mental health transformed their lives.

Several celebrities are embracing the role of advocate and lending support to mental health organizations. Phelps originally launched his eponymous foundation to promote water safety among children. However, the foundation expanded its scope to also promote physical and mental health, and Phelps has emerged as a leading mental health advocate in sport. The actress Glenn Close launched Bring Change 2 Mind to challenge the stigmatization of mental illness. Close started the foundation in 2010 after her sister was diagnosed with bipolar disorder and her nephew with schizoaffective disorder. "Every individual who speaks out inspires another. And another. That's how we'll end the stigma around mental illness," the organization's website states. Lady Gaga, an internationally renowned singer, started the Born This Way Foundation with her mother. The foundation supports mental health initiatives for youth, featuring youth-driven projects and educational programming. Finally, actress Taraji P. Henson started the Boris Lawrence Henson Foundation in 2018 to offer free therapy and to promote growth in the number of Black mental health professionals in the United States.

How are People Responding?

Michael Phelps described a moment before the COVID-19 pandemic when he spoke about mental health at a business meeting. An audience member stood up and, through tears, shared his own story. Phelps described the moment as awesome, and he believes in the power of one disclosure leading to another and another. When it comes to celebrities, he thinks "it's just going to get bigger and bigger."

The response to recent celebrity disclosures can be described as largely positive. When Love and DeRozan came out, researchers examined how social media users responded in 3,366 comments posted beneath the athletes' tweets. Fans praised the basketball stars for speaking up, offered words of encouragement and support, and even shared their own stories about mental health. "Keep your head up bro, we got your back," one fan responded. Another wrote, "It gets better." One fan thanked Love for being "a real man," and shared that he suffered severe anxiety for more than two decades. The fan said he, too, would be a real man, speak with his family, and seek treatment (Parrott et al., 2020).

Such comments are important because they normalize openness about mental health and provide readers hints about social norms concerning mental illness. As more people disclose, mental illness should be seen as more common and therefore less mysterious. We also look for clues about how people around us are thinking. What do people think about depression? How would society treat me if I shared my experience with depression? Given the amount of time we spend on social media, we might draw inference about societal attitudes based on how people respond to celebrities' disclosures.

Still, there are drawbacks for celebrities who openly advocate for mental health. A friend of Demi Lovato described how the persona of mental health advocate can be problematic: "It is a beautiful gift to be able to help people but at the same time, you become a martyr in a way that is so isolating, and I think it just gets to you" (Gold, 2021, para. 7).

What Effect?

Researchers have yet to figure out how celebrity disclosures affect people's attitudes, emotions, beliefs, and behaviors related to mental illness. Based on research in health communication, though, we might anticipate:

1. The more celebrities talk about mental health, the more common such conversations become.
2. A person who is hesitant to seek help might do so after a respected celebrity shares their own experience, including trials and recovery.
3. A person might be more willing to disclose their own story of mental illness after being inspired by a respected celebrity, which can challenge stigma and improve the person's own self-esteem.
4. A fan might pursue a specific form of treatment when it is praised by a celebrity they value.
5. One celebrity can inspire another star to disclose personal experience with mental illness, generating increased attention to the subject.

One research team studied young adults' attitudes toward treatment-seeking after Kevin Love's disclosure and found no significant results; however, the issue might have been in the study design (Towery et al., 2021). Other experiments showed promise. In the United States, Ferrari (2021) used abnormal psychology courses to test whether college students would express less stigma when celebrity disclosures were included in course lessons. As the course covered disorders, from severe depression to schizophrenia, Ferrari shared the disclosures of a celebrity affected by the condition. For example, while studying Obsessive Compulsive Disorder, students learned that the condition affected international soccer star David Beckham. When discussing bulimia nervosa, Ferrari shared the disclosure of American pop star Kesha. The psychology professor measured students' stigma levels before the lessons, after the lessons, and six months later, and compared the results to another group of students who completed a routine psychology course without celebrities. Students who encountered the celebrity examples expressed less stigmatizing attitudes and the effect lingered half a year later. The same could not be said for students who took the traditional course.

In addition to stigma reduction, celebrity disclosures nurture information-seeking and -sharing. After actor Robin Williams died by suicide, fans expressed remorse on social media, called for an end to stigma, and encouraged others to seek help if they needed it (Carpentier & Parrott, 2016). In South Korea, Lee conducted a novel study (2019a) in which he used online search queries, blog posts, and question/answer pages to see whether news stories about celebrities and panic disorders spurred information-seeking and -sharing. It appeared to do so, as news stories about celebrities and panic disorders were accompanied by increased searches, posts, and questions related to panic disorders between 2010 and 2015. In addition, Lee identified an increase in physician visits related to panic disorders that accompanied news stories about celebrities and the condition.

In a similar study, Lee (2019b) found that news stories about celebrity deaths by suicide were related to treatment-seeking rates among the Korean public. While previous studies focused on negative outcomes of coverage, including copycat deaths by suicide, Lee sought to understand whether any positive outcomes might emerge from the increased attention to mental illness. The data was correlational, so the study lacked insight into the reason psychiatrist visits would increase in the month after a celebrity's death by suicide. However, Lee reckoned that (a) the news coverage heightened people's personal concerns over their own depression or (b) people became more aware of depression and its potential outcomes. News stories about the celebrity deaths often included information about the symptoms of depression and ways it could be treated.

When Carrie Fisher died in 2016, fans used the hashtag #InHonorOfCarrie to discuss personal experiences with mental illness on the social media platform Twitter. By using hashtags, social media users can easily find other people who are conversing about a subject, in this case the passing of a famous actress and mental health advocate. More than 3.1 million tweets about Fisher appeared on December 27, 2016, the day she died. When Park and Hoffner (2020) studied 2,160 posts that used #InHonorOfCarrie, they found that people were thanking Fisher for her advocacy and sharing their own experiences with depression, bipolar disorder, and other illnesses. The conversation appeared positive, as people shared stories of treatment, recovery, and pride. One user wrote, "Thanks, Carrie for teaching me to accept myself," while another wrote, "My PTSD was so severe docs said I would never go to college or hold down a job. Today I have a degree and a career" (Park & Hoffner, 2020, p. 8).

Good research answers the question "Why?" Why, we might ask, do people pay attention to celebrities when other mental health advocates have been communicating similar messages for years? Studies in the field of persuasion offer a potential explanation. Celebrities are heuristic cues. They are novel, compared to the typical person, so we pay attention. This is the reason a professional basketball player sells car insurance. He is not an expert in the subject, though he probably does own and insure more vehicles than the average person. He is an attention-getter we hold in esteem. The insurance companies, car salesmen, shoe stores, and other sponsors hope that positive association will rub off on their product. In this regard, people pay attention when a celebrity discloses mental illness. In Hong Kong, Leung (2019) approached celebrity disclosure from the perspective of consumer persuasion research, wondering whether the credibility and familiarity one feels toward celebrities makes them persuasive when it comes to mental health. The researcher interviewed 35 college students to see whether they recalled a celebrity sharing personal experience with major depressive disorder; the reason they felt the celebrity disclosed; and whether they learned anything about the disorder through news coverage of the celebrity. At times, participants expressed cynicism, questioning whether the celebrities simply wanted publicity. In other instances, fans of the celebrity said they did indeed learn about symptoms of major depressive disorder through the news coverage.

An alternative—or supplementary—explanation involves the phenomenon of *identification*. When mental illness affects someone held in high esteem, fans can feel as though someone "close to them" is experiencing mental illness. Typical people identify with celebrities, seeing themselves in people who have experienced success most people only aspire to achieve. A teenager who loves basketball and looks up to DeMar DeRozan might say, "Wow. If it can happen to him, then it can happen to anybody."

Researchers in India (Jain et al., 2017) examined how fans' parasocial relationships with Bollywood actress Deepika Padukone affected their reactions to her experience with depression. In 2015, Padukone, her family, and her doctors described her experience with depression and stigma during an hour-long program on a major television network that targeted middle class, educated Indians in metropolitan areas. After the disclosure, the research team surveyed respondents' parasocial relationships with Padukone, intentions to pursue mental health care, and efficacy toward seeking treatment. The more people were exposed to Padukone, the more they perceived a relationship with the actress. The closer they felt to her, the more confident they felt in successfully pursuing treatment. The importance of the finding is underscored by the prevalence of depression in India, the nation with the highest rates in the world (Jain et al., 2017).

In an American study, Hoffner and Cohen (2018) surveyed adults following the death by suicide of Robin Williams. The extent to which respondents felt they "knew" Williams through parasocial interaction predicted less desire for social distance from people with depression. Meanwhile, the more people watched news of Williams' death, the greater they supported public mental health resources. Finally, the more people encountered news stories about Williams' accomplishments, the less they endorsed stereotypes about depression. In terms of behavior, people expressed greater willingness to seek treatment, share mental health information, and offer other people mental health support when they held parasocial relationships with Williams before his death.

Conclusion

A growing number of actors, artists, athletes and other celebrities are publicly sharing their experiences with mental illness. The disclosures illustrate the humanity behind celebrities while also challenging stereotypes and prejudice of mental illness. Celebrity disclosures can educate the public about mental health, advocating healthy behavior. Celebrities often bypass traditional media outlets when sharing their mental health, nurturing dialogue.

Not only are celebrities sharing, they often welcome the role of mental health advocate. When people open social media accounts, they are asked to share information about who they are. What do you do for a living? What are your favorite hobbies?

Michael Phelps has a Twitter account, and he describes himself as

1. Husband
2. Father, and
3. Mental health advocate

References

Calhoun, A. J., & Gold, J. A. (2020). "I feel like I know them": The positive effect of celebrity self-disclosure of mental illness. *Academic Psychiatry, 44*(2), 237–241.

Corrigan, P. W., & Rao, D. (2012). On the self-stigma of mental illness: Stages, disclosure, and strategies for change. *The Canadian Journal of Psychiatry, 57*(8), 464–469.

Ferrari, A. (2021). The persistence of stigma reduction after teaching abnormal psychology using celebrity narratives. *Teaching of Psychology, 48*(3), 191–196.

Gold, J. (2021). In her new documentary, Demi Lovato says being a mental health advocate almost killed her. *InStyle.* https://www.instyle.com/beauty/health-fitness/demi-lovato-documentary-mental-health-advocate

Hoffner, C. A., & Cohen, E. L. (2018). Mental health-related outcomes of Robin Williams' death: The role of parasocial relations and media exposure in stigma, help-seeking, and outreach. *Health Communication, 33*(12), 1573–1582.

Jain, P., Pandey, U. S., & Roy, E. (2017). Perceived efficacy and intentions regarding seeking mental healthcare: Impact of Deepika Padukone, a Bollywood celebrity's public announcement of struggle with depression. *Journal of Health Communication, 22*(8), 713–720.

Lee, S. Y. (2019a). The effect of media coverage of celebrities with panic disorder on the health behaviors of the public. *Health Communication, 34*(9), 1021–1031.

Lee, S. Y. (2019b). Media coverage of celebrity suicide caused by depression and increase in the number of people who seek depression treatment. *Psychiatry Research, 271*, 598–603.

Leung, V. S. (2019). The disclosure of celebrity major depressive disorder diagnoses in Hong Kong: Its effects on public awareness and understanding toward the illness. *Community Mental Health Journal, 55*(1), 120–128.

Love, K. (2020). To anybody going through it. *The Player's Tribune.* https://www.theplayerstribune.com/articles/kevin-love-mental-health

Park, S., & Hoffner, C. A. (2020). Tweeting about mental health to honor Carrie Fisher: How# InHonorOfCarrie reinforced the social influence of celebrity advocacy. *Computers in Human Behavior, 110*, 1–10.

Roberts, K. (2018). 39 celebrities who have opened up about mental health. *Harper's Bazaar.* https://www.harpersbazaar.com/celebrity/latest/g15159447/celebrities-depression-anxiety-mental-health/

Singh, O. (2020). 35 celebrities who have opened up about their struggles with mental illness. *Insider.* https://www.insider.com/celebrities-depression-anxiety-mental-health-awareness-2017-11

Towery, N. A., Buzzelli, N. R., Parrott, S., Billings, A. C., & Coombs, D. S. (2021). The power of love. In K. A. Brown, A. C. Billings, & M. Lewis (Eds.), *Revolution of the modern sports fan* (pp. 103–121). Lexington Books.

7

Meet John: Using Mediated Contact to Challenge Stereotypes

During mental health week, Buzzfeed News shared a video on YouTube in which men and women described what it feels like when you have a mental disorder (Buzzfeed, 2015). The video began, "Depression feels like _______."

"When I'm depressed, trying to do anything feels like trying to start a car when there's no gas in the car," says one young woman. "You can really want to go somewhere. You can want to do the thing, but you literally don't have the means."

The camera cuts to a young man wearing a button-up shirt. As he smiles, he explains that "depression to me feels like a giant weight, kind of like one of those big dumbbells. It starts in your gut, and you just feel it slowly intensify."

The video, titled "Living with a mental disorder," generated more than 2 million views on YouTube. More than 50,000 people liked the video, and 5,000 people left comments in which they did everything from sell herbal medicine to disclose personal experience with depression, anxiety, and ADHD. Most important, the video permitted people who are curious about depression and anxiety to "meet" someone who has personally walked the path. In establishing such contact, the news video potentially educated viewers, challenged stereotypes, and humanized depression and anxiety.

The video—and others like it—represent a promising avenue by which mental illness stigma may be challenged: parasocial contact. Social psychologists have long valued the power of intergroup contact in combating prejudice and discrimination (Paluck et al., 2019). The ever-growing presence of mass media in our daily lives is revealing the potential for a version of contact in which social groups never actually connect in-person. This *parasocial* contact occurs when members of different social groups meet through television shows, social media, movies, and news stories. Parasocial contact may occur when people communicate with one another, as with social media, or it may occur when one side (say an actor) is not cognizant of the other (a home television viewer). The key ingredient is the connection between two social groups, and as this chapter illustrates, the experience can change beliefs, reduce prejudice, and nurture empathy.

What is Contact?

Contact is a pillar of prejudice reduction; indeed, the existing evidence has led some researchers to definitely declare its effectiveness (Paluck et al., 2019). Contact is one of three primary ways activists have challenged the stigmatization of mental illness, complimenting education and protest. Put simply, contact occurs when one or more members of a marginalized group meets people from another social group. To illustrate, a mentally healthy person might hold inaccurate assumptions about major depression because they never met an individual affected by the illness. Their ignorance could be alleviated by having positive contact with a person who has navigated life with major depression.

Gordon Allport, an influential social psychologist, described the potential of contact in his seminal text *The Nature of Prejudice* (1954). Key factors inform the extent to which contact succeeds in reducing stereotypes, prejudice, and discrimination. In-group and out-group members should enjoy equal status, share common goals, cooperate, and work under the support of authorities, laws, or customs. Most important is Allport's statement that contact should nurture "the perception of common interests and common humanity between members of the two groups" (p. 281).

Fifty years after the publication of *The Nature of Prejudice*, Thomas F. Pettigrew and Linda R. Tropp reviewed more than 500 studies that tested the effects of intergroup contact (2016). Overall, the authors concluded, intergroup contact is an effective method for reducing prejudice and hostility between two groups. Another team of researchers (Paluck et al., 2019) supplemented the original meta-analysis with studies completed after its publication. The authors determined that the target of prejudice—such as race, gender, or mental illness—influences the extent to which contact is successful in reducing prejudice. Mental illness is one area in which contact appears to be particularly effective in mitigating prejudice, the authors concluded.

To illustrate, researchers in California wanted to see whether people's attitudes toward mental illness would change based on whether they encountered a person with mental illness in the real world compared to an anti-stigma or media program (Shearer, et al., 2021). The researchers reached out to more than 1,000 people, gauging whether they would want to live next door to someone with mental illness. A year later, they reached out again. Contact seemed to work. People who met someone affected by mental illness—including family and friends—were more willing to have one as a neighbor.

What is Parasocial Contact?

Informed by the contact hypothesis, media researchers developed the term "parasocial contact" to describe the phenomenon of meeting out-group members through television, movies, news stories and other mass media. Edward Schiappa, Peter B. Gregg, and Dean E. Hewes (2006) pioneered the research in the mass communication field, focusing on the potential role of prime-time television in reducing prejudice toward homosexual men. In a 2006 study, the researchers investigated whether viewing the U.S. television program *Will & Grace* could challenge prejudice. The situation comedy was described as groundbreaking when it first aired in 1998 because two main characters were openly gay. Critics initially challenged the characters as stereotypical, but the program also received praise for improving public opinion about the LGBT community. Joe Biden, while vice president of the United States, said the show "probably did more to educate the American public than almost anything anybody has ever done" (Eldridge, 2012). The research team surveyed 245 university students and found that the more they watched the show, the less they endorsed prejudice. The relationship was strongest for people who lacked real-world social contact with lesbians and gay men.

Since the study, researchers have collected additional evidence to show that the mass media can reduce prejudice by connecting audiences with positive examples of stigmatized people. As Chapter 6 described, people who lack first-hand experience with mental illness may learn about it by following the lives of athletes, actors, musicians, and other celebrities. People who are affected by mental illness are stereotyped as lacking success in personal and professional lives. Mental illness can also be misunderstood as weakness. When fans meet a successful athlete who has depression, the parasocial contact can contradict these existing beliefs: the athlete is clearly strong; the athlete reached the pinnacle of professional success, reaping benefits such as million-dollar contracts; and the athlete may appear socially successful because of well-publicized romantic relationships, friendships, and massive social media followings.

When confronted with the stereotype challenging information, the fan could (a) ignore the new information, (b) consider the celebrity an outlier when it comes to mental illness, or (c) reassess their existing beliefs. The more celebrities speak out, the less inclined the fan should be to discount the athlete's experience as an oddity. In addition to shifting thoughts, the fan could experience increased empathy for people who experience mental illness. After all, depression has affected someone they "know."

Beyond testimonials, contact can occur through fictional content such as television shows, movies, and novels. *Monk*, an American television show, immersed viewers in the life of Adrian Monk, a detective with obsessive compulsive disorder. The comedic drama lasted seven seasons, winning awards for reducing stigma by providing audiences a humanizing portrait of mental illness. While Monk demonstrated symptoms of mental illness—an obsessive aversion to germs, for instance—he was also skilled at his job and had friends. The show had its critics, who questioned whether it perpetuated stereotypes about OCD, but research suggests it was successful in challenging stigma. For example, researchers sought to understand how viewers' perceived relationships with Monk affected their attitudes toward mental illness in general (Hoffner & Cohen, 2015). The greater the perceived relationship, the less likely viewers were to endorse stereotypes about mental illness and the less likely they were to desire social distance from people with mental illness.

There is ample opportunity for mass media researchers to explore the processes and outcomes related to parasocial contact. For example, the timing of contact could be important, given the "invisible" nature of mental illness. Mental illness is often a concealable condition, one a person can keep hidden from others. This introduces the possibility of an outgroup member (e.g., a person with depression) being first considered an in-group member (e.g., a friend). The existing relationship could inform subsequent judgments of the person. For example, Robin Williams was an actor and comedian who was beloved for his roles as the genie in the Disney movie *Aladdin*, a kind-hearted doctor in *Patch Adams*, and other roles. Williams was known for his energetic personality, but the magnetism masked a history of severe depression. Williams died by suicide in 2014. The news was devastating for many fans, as they had essentially grown up with Williams as an ever-present celebrity figure. Although Williams was fairly open about his mental health, the news shocked fans who essentially experienced contact in retrospect. In other words, rather than meeting a person whose story challenges stereotypes, fans learned that an important persona in their lives had experienced mental illness all along.

Researchers examined young adults' responses to the news of Williams' death, finding that people were motivated to seek out information about depression. The news also reinforced for young adults that depression is an illness that "can happen to anyone," (Carpentier & Parrott, 2015). Cynthia Hoffner and Elizabeth Cohen (2018) found that people who held stronger parasocial relationships with Williams reported less desire for social distance from people with mental illness and greater willingness to seek treatment for depression. They also reported greater desire to help others who are affected by depression and/or suicidal thoughts.

Changing Beliefs, Eliciting Empathy

There are several reasons parasocial contact is an appealing tool for stigma reduction. First, the nature of mass media permits mental health advocates to quickly disseminate video testimonials to large audiences, as illustrated by the Buzzfeed News video described at the beginning of the chapter. Second, the creation and distribution of video-based testimonials are more affordable in terms of time and money when compared to live contact interventions (Tippin & Maranzan, 2019). Parasocial contact also affords greater control over the content and presentation style of the information being conveyed through the contact experience.

Similar to traditional contact, parasocial contact interventions appear to be successful in generating two key outcomes associated with stigma reduction. First, parasocial contact may challenge a target's traditional notions concerning mental illness, shaping beliefs and prejudice. Researchers in the United States (Wong et al., 2017) wanted to determine whether a disclosure by singer Demi Lovato could reduce stereotypes and social distance related to bipolar disorder. In an experiment, the researchers used different mediums (e.g., television, print) to provide participants contact with Lovato in which she discussed her experience with mental illness. Compared to a control group, participants did indeed finish the study endorsing fewer stereotypes and desiring less social distance from people affected by bipolar disorder.

Second, parasocial contact might nurture empathy for people affected by mental illness. Empathy is an emotion in which one person can understand and share the feelings of another (Oxford Dictionary, 2021). In Canada, Gregory K. Tippin and K. Amanda Maranzan tested an intervention in which people used an application called PhotoVoice to document their experiences with mental illness. The researchers split 303 university students into two groups. One watched the video testimonials, while the other group watched an unrelated video. The testimonials elicited empathic concern from viewers, which in turn predicted less stigmatizing attitudes toward people with mental illness. The effect appeared to linger for at least several weeks, as one month after the intervention, students reported a decreased desire to maintain social distance from people with mental illness.

In Germany, Marlene Hecht and colleagues (2021) conducted an experiment in which they tested whether one-time exposure to video testimonials could generate empathy and reflective thinking about a person with schizophrenia (which was featured in the first video) and autism (featured in the second video). Reflective thinking is captured in such statements as "this was thought-provoking." In the end, the research team found that exposure to the video about autism elicited empathy, which promoted increased reflective thinking. In turn, reflective thinking predicted positive attitudes toward people with mental illness in general.

Over time, repeated contact might nurture what researchers call a *parasocial relationship*, in which people feel as though they know a media character, celebrity, or other persona. As with contact, parasocial relationships challenge prejudice toward stigmatized groups and even nurture help-seeking behavior for stigmatized conditions. For example, the Hall of Fame basketball player Earvin "Magic" Johnson disclosed he had HIV during a 1991 press conference. In the wake of the announcement, health officials documented an uptick in the number of heterosexual men who sought testing for HIV. The disclosure appeared to challenge traditional notions that HIV did not affect heterosexual men. Researchers have found that Johnson's disclosure elicited stronger emotional reactions and help-related information seeking and behavior among people who held strong parasocial relationships with the basketball star. In other words, people who felt they knew Johnson experienced the type of distress one might feel upon learning a family member or close friend suffered a negative life event.

As described in Chapter 1, stigma presents a common barrier to mental health, as people might avoid seeking help or disclosing symptoms for fear of being labeled mentally ill or encountering prejudice. Critical attitudes toward mental health care might present an additional barrier. Given these challenges, Eric E. Rasmussen and David R. Ewoldsen (2016) investigated the potential for a popular talk show to nurture positive attitudes toward mental health treatment. The show, *Dr. Phil*, regularly drew millions of viewers and appeared on 200 television stations in the United States in the 2010s. In the study, the research team surveyed 306 parents or guardians of children ages 8–17. Half the participants were asked to watch a 12-minute clip from Dr. Phil's episode "Anorexic and Drug Addicted: Saving Morgan," in which the host counseled a girl and her parents in relation to her depression, drug abuse, and suicidal ideations. Half the participants did not watch the show. In the end, the one-time exposure (compared to none) had no effect. However, people who regularly watched the show reported stronger parasocial relationships with Dr. Phil. In turn, these relationships buoyed people's confidence that they could seek mental health treatment—and it would be effective—for themselves or their children. Finally, this efficacy predicted greater intentions to actually follow through and seek treatment for the parents or their children.

Technological Innovation & Contact

The opportunity to meet people from stigmatized social groups is greater than ever because of technological innovations. The early 2000s witnessed the rise of social media, which has become omnipresent in modern life. The internet also provides us the opportunity to share personal stories through websites, blogs, and online forums. Video games now represent one of the largest genres of entertainment in the world, and activist designers are embracing opportunities to connect gamers with characters affected by mental illness. Finally, average people can afford virtual reality equipment once relegated to the confines of million-dollar research and development labs. As Chapter 11 illustrates, the proliferation of gaming technology affords users the chance to not only "meet" a person with mental illness, but to virtually walk a mile in their shoes.

The world of social media can be toxic, to say the least, but for all its problems, social media permit people who would not otherwise meet to connect and learn about one another, reinforcing the commonalities of the human experience. Social media users can establish parasocial contact with people who share stories about life with depression, anxiety, and even severe disorders such as schizophrenia. They can ask questions, engage in dialogue, or simply learn about the person's life by following them on Facebook, Twitter, or another platform.

Of course, the contact could backfire if the follower's misguided assumptions and prejudices are simply confirmed. However, if the contact provides counter stereotypical information, elicits empathy, or highlights the human instead of the illness, the contact may be fruitful for mitigating stigma. The importance of social media is underscored by the fact a user can immediately reach millions of people around the world. This means a teenager in rural west Alabama, USA, who is curious about depression can connect with a mental health activist in London and learn. Twenty years ago, a teen in the same rural community would face limited—if any—options for learning about mental health from someone with direct experience.

Chapter 8 discusses the importance of Reddit and other websites in connecting people who have a mental illness and permitting them access to others who experienced similar struggles and, hopefully, recovery. Like social media, question-and-answer boards also permit users to connect with people who have experienced mental illness. A review of the Mental Health thread on Reddit (r/mentalhealth), for example, shows people asking questions such as "What does depression feel like?" and "Is this normal, or a mental health concern?" Such forums provide an environment in which people can ask questions and receive answers while remaining anonymous. Reddit threads are monitored by moderators and fellow users, who can give the seal of approval to responses by "upvoting" them. The tools help ensure responses are helpful rather than harmful or stigmatizing. Responses may focus on the negative at times—"on a bad day, it feels like hell," one person responded when asked about depression—but overall the dialogues appear positive, humanizing, and counter-stereotypical: a necessary component if one wishes for contact to succeed.

In addition to human-to-human contact through social media, technological advancements have permitted new modes of storytelling to afford users parasocial contact with fictional mentally ill characters. An increasing number of designers are exploring the potential of video games to initiate contact with people who are affected by depression, anxiety, and other illnesses. David Mullor and colleagues (2019) investigated the potential of a serious game called *Stigma-Stop* in challenging stereotypes and prejudice. The research team compared participants' reactions after (a) playing the game, (b) meeting a mental health patient face-to-face, or (c) listening to a talk by a mental health professional. In the serious game, players interacted with four characters affected by different disorders, including schizophrenia, depression, bipolar disorder, and agoraphobia. Results were promising, as the interactive game resembled education and real-world contact in its ability to challenge stereotypes related to dangerousness, avoidance, and other prejudices.

As virtual reality equipment—or VR—becomes more affordable, researchers are exploring whether it can be used for prosocial outcomes such as prejudice reduction. Although the study focused on another social group, recent research suggests contact may pay off via virtual reality. In this study, a German researcher had participants play the popular video game *Skyrim* using either a 2D console (PlayStation) or VR equipment. In the game, players were asked to help a Black avatar named Amren find a sword. Or, they were simply asked by a White researcher to perform the cooperative task. When he first formulated the contact hypothesis, Gordon Allport stressed the importance of cooperation in contact. Cooperative tasks require in-group and out-group members to see each other as teammates rather than competition. Results from the VR study were promising. Compared to the control group, players who helped the character of Amren subsequently reported less prejudicial explicit attitudes toward Black people. However, the results warrant additional investigation, because the study found no differences in participants' *implicit* attitudes. This is significant because implicit attitudes are beyond one's conscious control—they are simply cognitive associations—while explicit attitudes are ones people openly express. After playing the game, participants may have simply understood the researcher's goal and answered subsequent questions in a way that would present them in the best (non-racist) light.

Conditions for Success: Humanizing & Counter-Stereotypical

Overall, there is empirical support that contact reduces prejudice between social groups (Zhou et al., 2019). Less attention has been paid to the conditions described by Allport that would support the strongest positive outcomes—equal status between groups, shared goals, intergroup cooperation, and the support of laws, customs, and authorities (Paluck et al. 2019). In addition, the contact experience should challenge stereotypes and illustrate the shared humanity of the people involved.

Lessons can be gleaned from research concerning other social groups, including a study by German researchers who were interested in how parasocial and vicarious contact affected attitudes toward refugees (Schemer & Meltzer, 2020).

In an experiment, the researchers exposed participants to a short news video in which refugees demonstrated negative behavior among themselves (alcohol abuse, aggression) and against people who represent German natives (physically assaulting what would represent a participant's in-group). The stereotype-confirming behavior embodied negative contact, and as expected, it backfired in terms of stigma reduction. In two experiments, participants expressed more negative attitudes toward refugees when they experienced negative parasocial or vicarious contact.

Chapter 11 discusses technological advancements such as virtual reality that permit people to "walk a mile in the shoes" of a person with mental illness but can be dangerous when the experiences focus on negative stereotypes. VR has also been used to initiate contact, with comparable results. Stelzmann and colleagues (2021) tested whether VR could mitigate stigma by virtually connecting research participants and an individual with schizophrenia. The research team showed participants one of two videos—one using VR, the other a traditional recording—in which a young man discussed his symptoms, daily experiences, and family travails. The research team wanted to know whether the VR-based contact could reduce anxiety while increasing social closeness, empathy, and benevolence toward people with schizophrenia. The VR experience failed while the traditional version succeeded. The research team reckoned VR users found the experience overwhelming and had trouble processing the actual content.

In addition to being positive, contact should avoid the outlier effect. In other words, advocates should ensure the person can represent the broader social group of "people with mental illness," instead of an abnormal member. Otherwise, people who are targeted by an intervention might simply dismiss the person as an inaccurate representation of people with mental illness.

Conclusion

Research suggests positive parasocial contact can challenge prejudice while nurturing empathy for people with mental illness. Additional scholarship is needed, though, as researchers remain unsure about the conditions in which media-based contact succeeds in challenging stigma or how long effects last. Even if effects are ephemeral, Henderson (2020) writes, they should be treated as short-term medication for long-term illnesses.

"The implication is that contact should be ongoing or repeated to continue to counter the ongoing influence of public stigma," Henderson writes (p. 738). "Such contact then begins to resemble having a relationship with someone with a mental health problem, which is strongly associated with having more stigma-related knowledge, more positive attitudes, and less desire for social distance."

References

Breves, P. (2020). Reducing outgroup bias through intergroup contact with non-playable video game characters in VR. *Presence, 27*(3), 257–273.

Buzzfeed. (2015). Living with a mental disorder. https://www.youtube.com/watch?v=ezI2W32yNg8

Eldridge, D. (May 6, 2012). Biden 'comfortable' with gay marriage, cites 'Will & Grace'. *The Washington Times.* https://www.washingtontimes.com/news/2012/may/6/biden-will-grace-educated-public-about-gays/

Hecht, M., Kloß, A., & Bartsch, A. (2021). Stopping the stigma. How empathy and reflectiveness can help reduce mental health stigma. *Media Psychology, 25*(3), 367–386.

Henderson, C. (2020). Commentary on "Effect of contact-based interventions on stigma and discrimination." *Psychiatric Services, 71*(7), 738–739.

Hoffner, C. A., & Cohen, E. L. (2015). Portrayal of mental illness on the TV series Monk: Presumed influence and consequences of exposure. *Health Communication, 30*(10), 1046–1054.

Mullor, D., Sayans-Jiménez, P., Cangas, A. J., & Navarro, N. (2019). Effect of a Serious Game (Stigma-Stop) on reducing stigma among Psychology students: A controlled study. *Cyberpsychology, Behavior, and Social Networking, 22*(3), 205–211.

Paluck, E. L., Green, S. A., & Green, D. P. (2019). The contact hypothesis re-evaluated. *Behavioural Public Policy, 3*(2), 129–158.

Rasmussen, E. E., & Ewoldsen, D. R. (2016). Treatment via television: The relation between watching Dr. Phil and viewers' intentions to seek mental health treatment. *Journal of Health Communication, 21*(6), 611–619.

Schemer, C., & Meltzer, C. E. (2020). The impact of negative parasocial and vicarious contact with refugees in the media on attitudes toward refugees. *Mass Communication and Society, 23*(2), 230–248.

Schiappa, E., Gregg, P. B., & Hewes, D. E. (2006). Can one TV show make a difference? A Will & Grace and the parasocial contact hypothesis. *Journal of Homosexuality, 51*(4), 15–37.

Shearer, A. L., Roth, E., Cefalu, M. S., Breslau, J., McBain, R. K., Wong, E. C., . . . & Collins, R. L. (2021). Contact with persons with mental illness and willingness to live next door to them: Two waves of a California survey of adults. *Psychiatric Services, 72*(1), 23–30.

Stelzmann, D., Toth, R., & Schieferdecker, D. (2021). Can intergroup contact in virtual reality (VR) reduce stigmatization against people with schizophrenia? *Journal of Clinical Medicine, 10*(13), 2961.

Tippin, G. K., & Maranzan, K. A. (2019). Efficacy of a Photovoice-based video as an online mental illness anti-stigma intervention and the role of empathy in audience response: A randomized controlled trial. *Journal of Applied Social Psychology, 49*(6), 381–394.

Wong, N. C., Lookadoo, K. L., & Nisbett, G. S. (2017). "I'm Demi and I have bipolar disorder": Effect of parasocial contact on reducing stigma toward people with bipolar disorder. *Communication Studies, 68*(3), 314–333.

Zhou, S., Page-Gould, E., Aron, A., Moyer, A., & Hewstone, M. (2019). The extended contact hypothesis: A meta-analysis on 20 years of research. *Personality and Social Psychology Review, 23*(2), 132–160.

8

People Like Me: How Social Media Can Connect Us with Communities

It's 12 p.m. on the East coast.

A woman logs into her reddit account and visits the community /r/depression, an online message board offering peer support for people who experience depression, "because nobody should be alone in a dark place." The woman—referred to as Georgia here—is in a dark place.

She types the title for her thread: Alone.

Then she shares, expressing herself to an anonymous community of 824,000 people. She always felt alone, ever since childhood, and the feeling lingers now as she feels distance between herself and her family, friends, romantic partner. No one speaks to her. No one seems to care.

A person responds: You've got us.

A second: How are you? How is your day?

A third: I feel the same way, too.

A fourth, a fifth, a sixth. Within hours, dozens respond to the initial post, showing empathy, reassuring the woman she is not alone, sharing personal experiences that echo the ones she is navigating.

The thread represents a growing trend in mental health. People are finding emotional support, social connection, practical advice, and other helpful encounters through peer-to-peer support on social media, blogs, smartphone applications, and other Internet-based technology. Both mental health consumers and professionals are praising the developing area of healthcare access, describing information-seeking, -sharing, and health-related social connection as one positive byproduct of the ever-growing presence of social media in modern society.

Risks are inherent in using technology for mental health. Indeed, researchers have tempered the praise for online mental health communities by warning about negative outcomes (e.g., Lawlor & Kirakowski, 2014). In addition, many people lack access to the Internet or connected devices, which limits their ability to connect with online support communities or medical professionals via video services such as Zoom or FaceTime. Other people are concerned about privacy and the personal information collected by applications, social media platforms, and other technology developed by international corporations and surveilled by the government.

Still, as this chapter illustrates, peer-to-peer support via online devices shows promise for mitigating stigma. Under certain circumstances, peer support can weaken the threat of stigma on self-esteem (e.g., Verhaeghe et al., 2008). Online communities also appear able to buoy community members' mental health when they receive helpful, individualized, and positive comments from other community members (e.g., Saha & Sharma, 2020). Although fellow users might dole out bad medical advice—a serious concern—analyses of online forums suggest people often seek out and find "me too" moments in which they connect with people who can sympathize (e.g., Giles & Newbold, 2010). Such connection might be lacking in the real world, where mental illness is often stigmatized.

People define peer-to-peer support in different ways. Peer support can be a paid interaction, where a trained individual who also experienced mental illness offers counseling. Here, we focus on informal peer support. It occurs when people connect via social media, blogs, or even face-to-face to share experiences, lessons learned, and other conversation about mental illness. The chapter primarily focuses on the positive interpersonal outcomes of these communities, which provide social connection to people who might otherwise feel excluded from society—in other words, stigmatized. Informal peer support can challenge stigma through education, sharing knowledge concerning symptoms, treatment, and what it is like to live with depression, anxiety, or another condition. It can also simply offer support for one's morale during difficult times. As with any mass media, it is important to note that online peer support can be problematic at times. People might become too dependent on online communities, feeding into social avoidance and worsening mental health. People might receive bad medical advice, with life-threatening consequences. People might even encounter trolls, those online creatures who enjoy making other people feel bad.

Nevertheless, informal peer support has been around for decades, perhaps centuries according to scholars who date it to the 1800s in France (Shalaby & Agyapong, 2020). With technological advances, peer-to-peer support has become an increasingly common supplement to professional mental health care. People can connect with peer support professionals though smartphones and apps. In addition, they can seek out informal support through social media channels such as Reddit, Facebook, YouTube, and Twitch.

The platforms differ. Reddit provides anonymous message boards, while Facebook groups often include identifiable members. People can watch video testimonials and livestreams on YouTube, joining conversations by commenting on videos or in-stream chats. Twitch often features video gamers who converse with followers during live streams. Although they differ, the platforms share commonalities: they can help people connect with kindred spirits, and they can foster a sense of community.

Such benefits were documented by Ailsa McLellan and colleagues at the University of Victoria in Canada (2022) when they studied 985 comments beneath 20 YouTube videos about mental illness stigma. Comments built community, the researchers said, and they shared personal experience with mental illness. They challenged traditional notions of mental health, including diagnoses, and they also challenged stigma. Finally, commenters offered others explanations for mental illness.

Community and social connection are important for mental health. People who experience depression, social anxiety, and other conditions may feel isolated, unable to positively connect with friends, family, romantic partners, or people in general (e.g., Zlotnick et al., 2000). Online communities can provide an alternative method for connection, one in which people can open up without fear of real-world consequences such as stigma.

Researchers are paying extra attention to the outcomes of online peer support given its increasing popularity outside the professional world of mental health. People are telling researchers that these platforms provide a sense of community that reduces isolation and inspires hope. Given the positive outcomes, experts are recommending we "seize the opportunity" in relation to online peer-to-peer support, as "social media will empower consumers to link up and transform the nature of the services they are receiving" (Alvarez-Jimenez et al., 2016).

This chapter describes how people are using online media and peer support to challenge stigma, especially stigma toward oneself. It focuses on four positive outcomes of online peer support: finding community, reducing isolation, sharing personal experience and advice, and providing a safe space for discussions that can feel too difficult for face-to-face conversation.

A Sense of Community

Isolation can be an issue, to say the least, when it comes to mental illness. People can feel alone because they feel unable to connect with friends, family, or coworkers. They can feel as though no one understands what they are going through. This sense of isolation can be the product of mental illness, and also a cause of depression and other conditions.

Thanks to social media, people are able to find online communities which provide a sense of belonging they might not otherwise experience in the offline world. Also, the conversations can occur over shared passions, such as video games, trading cards, or sports. To illustrate, millions of people watch others play video games on the popular platform Twitch, which permits viewers to see (a) the person gaming, (b) the video game as it is played, and (c) and a feed in which viewers can post notes to the gamer. Although video games remain the focus, Twitch has provided a route by which people who are interested in gaming can build communities and engage in serious conversations. This includes conversations about mental health.

Inspired by these conversations, Reesha Gandhi and colleagues at the New Jersey Institute of Technology (2021) interviewed two dozen Twitch viewers who had witnessed conversations about mental health. The gamers said the disclosures come in many shapes and sizes. At times they are spontaneous, prompted by comments from the streamer or one of the viewers. At other times, streamers actually invite trained counselors and other special guests onto the live feed; an informed dialogue about mental health can occur while viewers also watch gameplay. As with other peer support, gamers described good advice—and terrible advice—being doled out by the streamers to viewers who were struggling. In one exceptional instance, after a follower donated his "last" dollars toward the streamer, the streamer stopped gameplay, encouraged the person to call the suicide prevention hotline and moderated a conversation about mental health. People often appreciate peer support when they are going through a difficult time; it need not come from a group devoted to mental health.

Still, it does help to connect with people who have experienced comparable ordeals. In Australia, Anne Williams and colleagues (2018) studied whether videos of "lived experience" could help people who experience psychosis. The research team uploaded videos onto an interactive website in which people could find information about recovery, stress management, relationships, and other helpful tips for living with psychosis. The team asked people who had experience with psychosis to watch the videos either alone or with a mental health worker. For example, in one video, a woman described her experiences taking medication and how they help her manage her mental health. Website visitors were invited to share their own stories in comments beneath the videos.

"Quite a few of my illnesses, they actually do make you feel quite, quite alone a lot of the time," one person said. "For me to be able to see that there were other people out there struggling just as much as I was . . . was quite helpful" (p. 6).

Another responded, "I don't have to through it by myself" (p. 6).

Researchers in the United Kingdom interviewed members of a Facebook group for alopecia areata, an autoimmune condition characterized by hair loss (Iliffe & Thompson, 2019). The condition can affect people's mental health, nurturing depression and anxiety. The researchers interviewed 11 women who used Facebook pages organized by Alopecia UK. The women described finding emotional support through the site: "It's nice when ladies post pictures of new wigs," one woman wrote. "I decided to try a different style from seeing a post, and I love it. I posted a picture wearing a new wig and I got so many positive comments, which was nice." Another wrote, "It feels more normal now I see others who look like me, whereas before this group the only bald person I saw was me at home alone in front of the mirror." The women described a reduced sense of isolation, which buoyed their mental health: "In the beginning I couldn't go out, wouldn't look in the mirror, became withdrawn and was probably very depressed. Since joining the group I have realized that it's OK to be different."

The benefits of online communities can extend beyond mental health. For example, Naslund and colleagues (2016) explored the potential of a social media group designed to help people with severe mental illness adopt—and maintain—healthy eating and exercise habits. Over six months, nine people exercised, ate healthy, tracked achievements using wearable technology, and provided each other support and success stories over a private Facebook group.

You Are Not Alone

Helen M. Farrell, a Harvard-trained psychiatrist, reached nearly 19 million viewers with her YouTube video "What is depression?" Posted on the TED-ED channel, the video teaches viewers about symptoms and treatments for depression (Ted-Ed, 2015). The video elicited 24,000 comments, including this statement: "Depression is like having a mind that wants to die, but a body that wants to live." The statement received 25,000 likes and generated additional conversation from other viewers. "I can feel this," one person wrote. "Oh my God. This statement is what I have been feeling for years but could never put in words."

The commentary illustrates an additional benefit of social media channels. People can recognize they are not alone in their struggles. People can feel weird or different when they experience mental illness, even though depression, anxiety, and other conditions are common. The sense of being different, in turn, can exacerbate negative feelings and thoughts about oneself, feeding self-stigma. Online peer support can illustrate that others are affected, too, and they can empathize.

For example, the teenage years can be emotionally trying for anyone. They can be especially stressful for people who identify as LGBTIQ because of stigma, prejudice, and discrimination. In Australia, Paul Byron and colleagues sought to understand how LGBTIQ teenagers were connecting with others for emotional support. In the study, teenagers described peers and online resources as key sources of information and support related to mental health. As one 19-year-old female told the researchers, friends who also have anxiety "help me assess my own thoughts but also make me feel less alone and like I am not weird for feeling and thinking the way I do" (p. 31). Another teen told researchers they were able to connect with similar people they would not otherwise meet in real life (Byron et al., 2016).

Parents, politicians, and mental health experts often express concern over young people's use of social media (e.g., Guevara, 2022). Anna Lavis and Rachel Winter wondered whether the relationship between social media use and self-harm might be a bit more complicated than good/bad, harmful/helpful. The researchers studied how youths in the United Kingdom discussed self-harm on Twitter, Reddit, and Instagram. Lavis and Winter used interviews to supplement an analysis of 10,000+ social media posts and 36,000+ comments. Overall, they found, people often turned to social media for peer support, seeking help, understanding, and environments in which they were not stigmatized. Support could be sustained, as demonstrated on Reddit when one user disappeared from the board for an extended period of time, triggering another user to question the absence, leading other users to investigate. The person ultimately returned—blaming a hospital visit—and the community welcomed the person back. As the researchers note, this contrasts the users' descriptions of negative offline interactions.

In another study, researchers in the United Kingdom examined themes in 132 tweets with the hashtag #WhyWeTweetMH (Berry et al., 2017). The researchers identified four major themes. First, people described the platform as "the one space I can speak with people." Another person tweeted, "I am able to communicate with other people with the same experiences." A third person explained that they share mental health on Twitter "so I do not feel that I am the only person with MH concerns."

I've Been There. Here's What I Would Do

Internet users always run the risk of encountering bad information, from so-called "fake news" to terrible medical advice. Still, the Internet remains the go-to source for information when people are trying to figure out what ailment might be responsible for their pounding headache, sore throat, and stuffy ears. The same goes for bad moods that linger, emotional rollercoasters, or checking the stove to make sure it is off eight times before leaving the house.

Despite the risk of bad information, the Internet does provide people the opportunity to connect with others who have navigated life's challenges and emerged in better shape. When it comes to mental health, peers can offer guidance on the symptoms people are experiencing, what to watch out for when it comes to medication or therapy, and other bits of advice about navigating life with a mental illness. The advice can be helpful, especially when a person feels as though they have no one to consult in the "real" world.

To illustrate, researchers in the United States surveyed 135 Twitter users to better understand how they used social media for mental health information-seeking and -sharing (Naslund et al., 2017). The users all self-identified as having a mental illness. Nearly 7 in 10 (67%) described their main reason for using social media as connecting with other people who also have mental illness and sharing personal experience about living with mental illness. Often users spent time learning about mental illness from others and learning strategies for coping with mental illness.

Different motivations may guide people to use certain types of technology for mental health and wellbeing, as researchers in the United Kingdom discovered (Stawarz et al., 2019). The research team surveyed 81 people who used technology to care for their mental health. People used websites for recommendations on how to deal with daily stress and anxiety. Meanwhile, they turned to social media and discussion forums to encounter other other people's stories and glean insight into their own experiences.

People often find support for mental health through the shared stories of others. When Alexandra R. D'Agostino and colleagues studied 100 posts about opioid addiction on the popular social media platform Reddit, they found evidence of the value of stories. People sought advice and support from other people on the thread, and they received responses commonly found in group therapy: hope, validation, advice, and, most often, shared personal experience. Few of the comments, the researchers noted, contained bad advice. "This finding should work to alleviate concerns that online social support networks have the potential to do more harm than good among individuals who are seeking recovery from addiction," D'Agostino and colleagues explained (p. 7).

Online communities can develop the complexity of real-world brethren in several ways. The communities develop formal rules and social norms. People develop strategies for determining who to trust and when. To illustrate, in New Zealand, Kerry Gibson and Susanna Trnka used a novel approach to study how 22 people aged 16–21 use social media to give and receive support for emotional distress. First, the researchers interviewed the youths. They described how teens usually have more than one account on any given social media platform: One for close real-world friends, and another for the public. Language develops its own style: Teens pick up hints from friends, such as fewer happy posts or emojis, as indications the person might not be feeling great. In addition to interviews, the researchers collected screenshots of conversations the youths had with friends. The conversations demonstrated tact and consideration. "Hey man you want to talk," one person wrote a friend. "Thank u I'd rather not," the person responded. "Alright. I'll be up for a while longer if you change your mind." Technology can create an opportunity for "opening up" that might not otherwise emerge in face-to-face interaction.

Conclusion

Computer-mediated communication has introduced promising avenues by which people may support one another in relation to mental health. Although risks are inherent, including negative interactions and inaccurate information, social media, video-based conferencing platforms, and other digital tools are allowing people to connect, challenge stigma, and educate others about symptoms, treatment, and recovery related to mental health. Peer-to-peer support can benefit both the recipient and provider (see Shalaby & Agyapong, 2020). Providers can experience increased confidence and self-esteem, personal and professional growth, and a reframed sense of personal identity. Meanwhile, recipients can benefit from stigma reduction, empowerment, and nonjudgmental support.

References

Alvarez-Jimenez, M., Gleeson, J. F., Rice, S., Gonzalez-Blanch, C., & Bendall, S. (2016). Online peer-to-peer support in youth mental health: Seizing the opportunity. *Epidemiology and Psychiatric Sciences, 25*(2), 123–126.

Berry, N., Lobban, F., Belousov, M., Emsley, R., Nenadic, G., & Bucci, S. (2017). #WhyWeTweetMH: Understanding why people use Twitter to discuss mental health problems. *Journal of Medical Internet Research, 19*(4), e107.

Byron, P., Rasmussen, S., Wright Toussaint, D., Lobo, R., Robinson, K. H., & Paradise, B. (2017). 'You learn from each other': LGBTIQ Young People's Mental Health Help-seeking and the RAD Australia Online Directory.

Gandhi, R., Cook, C. L., LaMastra, N., Uttarapong, J., & Wohn, D. Y. (2021). An exploration of mental health discussions in live streaming gaming communities. *Frontiers in Psychology, 12*, 751.

Guevara, S. B. (2022). Senators introduce bill to limit harmful effects of social media on young people. ABC News. https://abcnews.go.com/Politics/senators-introduce-bill-limit-harmful-effects-social-media/story?id=82932781

Hollis, C., Sampson, S., Simons, L., Davies, E. B., Churchill, R., Betton, V., . . . & Tomlin, A. (2018). Identifying research priorities for digital technology in mental health care: Results of the James Lind alliance priority setting partnership. *The Lancet Psychiatry, 5*(10), 845–854.

Iliffe, L. L., & Thompson, A. R. (2019). Investigating the beneficial experiences of online peer support for those affected by alopecia: an interpretative phenomenological analysis using online interviews. *British Journal of Dermatology, 181*(5), 992–998.

Lavis, A., & Winter, R. (2020). # Online harms or benefits? An ethnographic analysis of the positives and negatives of peer-support around self-harm on social media. *Journal of Child Psychology and Psychiatry, 61*(8), 842–854.

Naslund, J. A., Aschbrenner, K. A., & Bartels, S. J. (2016). How people with serious mental illness use smartphones, mobile apps, and social media. *Psychiatric Rehabilitation Journal, 39*(4), 364.

Naslund, J. A., Aschbrenner, K. A., Marsch, L. A., & Bartels, S. J. (2016). Feasibility and acceptability of Facebook for health promotion among people with serious mental illness. *Digital Health, 2*, 2055207616654822.

Naslund, J. A., Aschbrenner, K. A., McHugo, G. J., Unützer, J., Marsch, L. A., & Bartels, S. J. (2019). Exploring opportunities to support mental health care using social media: A survey of social media users with mental illness. *Early Intervention in Psychiatry, 13*(3), 405–413.

Shalaby, R. A. H., & Agyapong, V. I. (2020). Peer support in mental health: Literature review. *JMIR Mental Health, 7*(6), e15572.

Stawarz, K., Preist, C., & Coyle, D. (2019). Use of smartphone apps, social media, and web-based resources to support mental health and well-being: Online survey. *JMIR Mental Health, 6*(7), e12546.

Ted-Ed. (2015). What is depression? Helen M. Farrell. YouTube. https://www.youtube.com/watch?v=z-IR48Mb3W0

Williams, A., Fossey, E., Farhall, J., Foley, F., & Thomas, N. (2018). Recovery after psychosis: Qualitative study of service user experiences of lived experience videos on a recovery-oriented website. *JMIR Mental Health, 5*(2), e9934.

Zlotnick, C., Kohn, R., Keitner, G., & Della Grotta, S. A. (2000). The relationship between quality of interpersonal relationships and major depressive disorder: Findings from the National Comorbidity Survey. *Journal of Affective Disorders, 59*(3), 205–215.

9

Protest: Calling for Change Via News and Social Media

The Scottish government recently launched an initiative to destigmatize alcohol and drug abuse, using advertisements to target misperceptions such as the notion that substance abuse is a lifestyle choice or moral weakness (Scottish Government, 2021). Ads protested terms such as "alcoholic" and "junkie," saying the labels could prevent people from admitting they need help. People should speak up when they hear hurtful comments, the ads declared, because protesting stigma could help more people pursue treatment.

The ads emerged as Scotland witnessed an uptick in the number of people dying or hospitalized for drug and alcohol issues. The nation's drug policy leader called the campaign "hard hitting," saying, "By addressing stigma, and the silence and alienation it causes, we make it easier for people to seek help and that is to the benefit of each and every one of us" (para. 8).

The campaign embraced a form of anti-stigma work called protest, which uses a more direct approach than education and contact by calling out instances of stigma as inappropriate. Education seeks to share accurate information about mental illness, while contact attempts to nurture empathy for people who are affected by mental illness. Protest challenges. Mental health advocates call out poor behavior and policy while demanding action from elected leaders, mental health providers, and fellow citizens. In the modern world, where activists can quickly and easily reach millions of people through social media, anti-stigma protests appear to be increasing. Protest may not be the best tool for changing people's attitudes, at times backfiring because people do not enjoy being told they are wrong. However, protest can be helpful for changing healthcare policy, eliciting action, and challenging stigmatization at the societal level.

This chapter discusses how protests have been conducted through mass media, focusing on news coverage and social media. Mental health activists can drum up attention from community journalists by using techniques described here. Meanwhile, social media can quickly shine a spotlight on issues by empowering grassroots activists. Social media is shifting the dynamics of modern social movements, including protests related to mental health and stigma.

What is Protest?

Protest is "a statement or action expressing disapproval of or objection to something," or "to declare firmly and emphatically in the face of stated or implied doubt" (Oxford English Dictionary, 2021). In politics, protest often involves marches, signs, motivational speakers, and demands for action.

Experts use terms such as "confront" and "tackle" when describing the need to mitigate stigma attached to mental illness (e.g., Mukadam & Livingston, 2012). Such language underscores the role of conflict and power in protests against stigma. Alastair Benbow (2007) describes protest as focused on "the enforcement of rights" for people with mental illness, including equal opportunities for work, education, housing, and legal protection. "The approach is underpinned by moral authority and need not depend on sympathy or understanding," Benbow writes (p. 34). "It stresses the 'right to be different,' with no need for persuasion or concealment; thus, it is not necessary for there to be a change in public attitudes."

Activists challenge traditional notions about mental illness that are rooted in power (Link & Phelan, 2001), and shifts in power are critical to ending stigma. As Deen Freelon and colleagues write (2018, p. 991), "power is an indispensable resource for social movements," defining the term as "the capacity to bring about desired changes in society." Power is also "the capability to intervene in a given set of events so as in some way to alter them" (Giddens, 1987, p. 7). Protest, then, demands that mental health advocates think about messaging, membership, and tact when challenging the existing beliefs of other people and institutions. Otherwise, protests can be off-putting and backfire. For example, David L. Penn and Shannon M. Couture (2002) cautioned against telling people to avoid buying into negative beliefs about mental illness. "Instructing individuals to ignore or suppress negative thoughts and attitudes towards a particular group can have paradoxical rebound effects," the researchers wrote (p. 20). "Stigma will be augmented rather than reduced."

Toward this end, experts recommend an approach that combines education and dialogue rather than conflict. To illustrate, an American politician found himself in hot water when he used terms related to suicide to discuss election outcomes (Associated Press, 2007). Mike Huckabee, who twice lost the Republican nomination for president, said his opponents might be "sitting in a warm tub of water with razor blades" (para. 2) because of their lack of support. The comment drew ire and led the American Foundation for Suicide Prevention to write an open letter that read (para. 10), "While we understand that these statements were meant to be humorous, they instead make light of suicide, and contribute to the myth that suicide is a rational choice rather than the fatal consequence of mental illness." Huckabee apologized. The open letter illustrates an educational approach to protesting a politician's derogatory references to mental health, which appear often in the comments of presidential candidates on social media and during debates (Parrott & Allen, 2021). Instead of condemning Huckabee as a human being or politician, calling names and levying insults, the Foundation's leadership protested the comment and educated people about the reason it could be harmful. Such tact avoids alienation and argument.

In addition to tact, protest requires patience and persistence, a continuous push to alter attitudes and institutions. The complex nature of mental illness stigma requires a multi-pronged approach in challenging it, and advocates have used protest to advocate for change in everything from governmental policy to the way people speak about mental illness. Protestors have organized letter writing, social media, and petition campaigns to challenge misinformation and stereotypes in the mass media. Benbow (2007, p. 35) underscores the need for persistence and multi-media approaches when challenging stigma with mass media. "The media is an immensely powerful machine," he writes. "In order for it to change opinions toward the mentally ill, it needs to be used in all its forms."

Researchers have sought to understand what makes protests successful in the fight against stigma. Rüsch and colleagues (2005) describe two key lessons learned from the work of German-based BASTA, which used email-based campaigns to protest stereotypes in advertising and other media. The lessons? Numbers and persistence. First, many people emailed the public relations department or "people in charge" of the company targeted by protestors. Second, BASTA maintained pressure by documenting its appeal (and the company's response) on its website.

Similar efforts were launched by the U.S.-based National Alliance on Mental Illness through its StigmaBusters campaign, in which the organization maintained a website by which followers could report and share mental illness stereotypes in commercials, news stories, movies, and other media fare. StigmaBusters produced results, as described by Corrigan and Gelb (2006). In one case, activists targeted *Wonderland*, a dramatic television program on ABC. In the first episode, a mentally ill man murdered random people and stabbed a pregnant psychiatrist in the stomach with a hypodermic needle. Members of StigmaBusters reached out to the television show's producers, network, and importantly, advertisers. ABC ultimately canceled the show.

Researchers have described protest as "reactive" (Mukadam & Livingston, 2012, p. 381). However, it need not be. Stigma-related issues are often entrenched in society and institutions, which means we can anticipate issues and be proactive. To illustrate, here are ways mental health advocates have used protests to call for change:

- In Michigan, activists gathered for an annual "Walk a Mile in My Shoes" rally. Thousands of people walked around the Capitol building before rallying on the front lawn to advocate for insurance parity, challenge stigma, and advocate for mental health care in a state where 300,000 people use behavioral health services. Through the rally, activists engaged politicians, drew public attention, and also elicited news coverage from television stations and news sites (CMHA, 2022).
- In Montana, protestors rallied outside the regional hospital to urge health officials to launch inpatient psychiatric care. Protestors included Glenn Close, an award-winning actress and mental health advocate who held a sign that read "Mental Health Empowers" (Loveridge, 2021).
- At West Virginia University, students protested the public institution's handling of mental health following the death by suicide of a student. Students shared stories about their own mental health and called for additional resources, citing a backlogged treatment center on campus (Ostrove, 2021).

Mass media are the reason these protests in Michigan, Montana, and West Virginia reached people outside their communities. Reporters covered the protests for community newspapers and television stations, and those stories were picked up by news aggregators (Google, Yahoo), wire services (Associated Press), and sibling publications within the same news company. The protests—and news coverage—were also shared via Facebook, Twitter, and other social media.

Mental health activists should appreciate the importance of mass media in protesting for change related to stigma. Using both news coverage and social media, advocates can increase attention toward causes while also applying public pressure to corporations, politicians, and other people in charge who might otherwise relegate mental health to the periphery.

To illustrate, the National Alliance on Mental Illness spearheaded a protest of the candy manufacturer Nestle USA in 1999 (Kezwer, 2000). NAMI and First Lady Rosalynn Carter (a prominent mental health advocate) called on followers to protest the company after it used derogatory language as monickers for a new line of candy—"Psycho Sam," "Looney Jerry," and "Weird Wally." NAMI described behind-the-scenes efforts of "quiet diplomacy" as failing, and therefore amplified the effort via the news media. On its website, NAMI called for an end to Nestle USA's use of the derogatory names. It also published an open letter to the CEO and chairman of Nestle in which NAMI focused on how the language could be problematic for children—referencing suicide, stigma, and the mass shooting at Columbine High School in Colorado—essentially pitting the worldwide conglomeration against children. Nestle backed off its original decision to keep the names after NAMI called on its StigmaBusters advocates to boycott the company. A spokesperson explained, "As with all businesses, we evaluate our brands and change business strategies based on consumer preferences and trends" (Kezwer, 2000).

News as a Tool for Mental Health Protest

As described in Chapter 4, a working knowledge of news values and routines can help mental health advocates better communicate messages that challenge stigma. Journalists report stories that demonstrate proximity, timeliness, conflict, impact, prominence, relevance, and other qualities. By pitching story ideas that embody these values, advocates stand greater chance of generating reporter interest. To illustrate, advocates who simply identify a need for mental health resources might drum up little attention from reporters. However, the idea could gain traction when situated within the broader narrative of the COVID-19 pandemic (or another timely issue), when communities across the United States witnessed increased demand for mental healthcare. This updated idea demonstrates impact (a large number of people are affected), timeliness (the issue is happening now), and relevance (people are thinking more about depression and anxiety than during typical time periods).

Local and regional reporters are generally easy to reach by telephone, email, social media, or even letter. An advocate who wants to pitch a story needs only to think through the newsworthiness of their idea, craft an argument centered around these news values, and share the idea with a reporter and/or editor for the community newspaper, television station, or radio station.

Understanding newsroom routines also helps. Journalists often face numerous deadlines each day, which means an individual reporter must focus on using time wisely. That means covering major newsworthy events quickly and accurately while meeting deadlines. When advocates are scheduling formal protests, they should consider the timing—a mid-morning protest might generate attention on the 12 o'clock news and later broadcasts (5, 6, 10 p.m.). However, a mid-morning protest also runs the risk of missing out on the evening news, which is more heavily watched, because journalists had an entire afternoon to cover other breaking news events. These new events could essentially push the morning protest off the evening line-up. In addition, it would be wise to consider the day of the week. The weekend shifts are usually understaffed in newsrooms, but the news cycle is also generally slower. A slower cycle means less competition for attention; however, any major stories could interfere with a reporter's ability to cover your protest.

Visual elements are incredibly important for protest stories. A story that gives journalists opportunities to take photos and/or videos should stand better chance of generating attention. Journalists face decisions each day in deciding what makes the front page of the newspaper, the 10 o'clock news, or the social media feed. In each instance, photos and videos increase a story's odds of making the cut. It could be a face-to-face interview, protestors holding signs, a tour of a mental health center—any number of visuals.

Advocates should bear in mind potential outcomes of the images. For example, a protest in which two people hold signs outside a clinic could communicate to the viewing audience that not many people are actually interested in the issue. Social movement experts also recommend the use of a spokesperson, when possible. The person should be comfortable communicating with journalists—on camera and off—and understand the professional routines of journalists. It would be wise to clearly identify achievable goals that can become recommendations or talking points. In other words, you could say "End the stigma," but what steps would that involve? By identifying concrete goals—"Everyone should use person-first language"—advocates can make desired outcomes more tenable.

In addition to story ideas, journalists are often accepting of constructive criticism. When journalists write, show, or say something inappropriate, advocates can connect the journalist in an educational way. For example, reporters might be less inclined to describe a game's end as "insane" if advocates communicate the reason such language is problematic. To illustrate, a Republican political pundit called a teenage activist a "mentally ill Swedish child" on national television while describing climate change as "hysteria" (Chiu, 2019, para. 2). A clip of the show went viral on social media, drawing condemnation. The executive director of the Autistic Self Advocacy Network called the comment "unconscionable" in an interview with *The Hollywood Reporter*, saying, "History is full of autistic people and people with other cognitive disabilities who were and are compelling, credible activists and leaders" (Barr, 2019, para. 7). Meanwhile, the executive director of the Asperger/Autism Network told the Reporter that "we know that individuals on the autism spectrum can use their strengths to make outstanding contributions to society because we see it every day with our community members" (para. 8). Fox News, which broadcasts the show, publicly apologized for the "disgraceful" comment and indicated it would not schedule the pundit again (Barr, 2019). Although the initial protest elicited action, Fox News backtracked and permitted the pundit to sell a book on the network (Bremner, 2021).

A similar case appeared in the UK in 2021, after Prince Harry and wife Meghan Markle were interviewed by Oprah Winfrey (Ritman, 2021). Markle, an actress, described having thoughts of suicide. A British talk show host known for making inflammatory statements questioned Markle's disclosure, saying "I wouldn't believe her if she read me a weather report." Mind, a mental health charity, protested the statement publicly via social media and with the television network, ITV. "It's vital that when people reach out for support or share their experiences of ill mental health that they are treated with dignity, respect and empathy," the organization shared with its 513,000 followers on Twitter. Nearly 100,000 people liked the post.

Social Media: Changing the Dynamics of Social Movements

The United States survived social turmoil during 2020–2021. The COVID-19 pandemic claimed nearly one million lives (CDC, 2022), nurtured social isolation, and produced the worst unemployment levels since World War II. A bitter presidential election concluded in November 2020, and supporters of the failed candidate attacked the nation's Capitol, killing five people. Throughout the year, smartphone videos captured police officers beating or shooting unarmed civilians. It is safe to say 2020–2021 jeopardized many Americans' mental health; indeed, health experts documented an increase in depression (Ettman, 2020).

It was during this period that a movement gained traction on social media. People used the hashtag #BlackMindsMatter more than 30,000 times to promote mental health among Black Americans and call for an end to stigma[1]. In September 2020, for example, Twitter users protested racism in the mental health profession during a week-long event in which Black people shared research, personal experience with mental health, and stories about what it means to be a person of color in the field of psychology.

#BlackMindsMatter is only one movement to harness the power of social media to protest the stigmatization of mental illness. Activists are capitalizing on the omnipresence of social media in modern life. In 2008, 2 in 10 Americans used social media. By 2020, 7 in 10 did so, presenting an opportunity for users to reach other people at a scale never before seen (Auxier & Anderson, 2021). Social media use is most common among teens and young adults, periods of life in which symptoms of mental illness often emerge and treatment begins (Kessler et al., 2007). At the time of writing, YouTube and Facebook were the most widely used platforms in the United States (Auxier & Anderson, 2021).

Social media shifted the structure of political movements—including anti-stigma protests—from structured and hierarchical organizations to broader, more inclusive efforts (e.g., Poell & van Dijck, 2018). Activists have used social media for mental health-related protests in the United States, Spain, United Kingdom, Australia, Denmark, and other countries (e.g., Betton et al., 2015). Scholars describe the phenomenon as one embracing a "bottom up," rather than "top down" approach.

As with other protests, social media-based protest can be particularly effective when it engages in education rather than confrontation. In the United Kingdom, Victoria Betton and colleagues (2015) described public protests after a national supermarket chain sold a "mental patient" Halloween costume. Twitter users responded by sharing "selfies," or photos of themselves, the statement "This is what a real mental patient looks like," and the hashtag #mentalpatient. The hashtag generated 6,694 posts in 24 hours, demonstrating the ability of social media protests to generate significant attention in a short period of time. Betton

1 The hashtag was also used to support the education of Black students.

and colleagues (p. 443) believed the protest created "a sense of solidarity, as well as minimizing a recognized limitation of 'direct contact,' namely discounting the experience of one or a few people as an exception, rather than the norm. When scores of people use a common hashtag, it may be harder to ignore or minimize their experience."

Collective social identities are instrumental in the success of political movements. The collective identity dubbed "persons with mental illness" has shifted from the shadows to the forefront of popular attention following the pandemic and the coming-out stories of professional athletes, actresses, musicians, and other celebrities. Bucking self-stigma, celebrities (and others) have strongly claimed the collective identity of "a person with depression," or "a person with anxiety," sharing the lived experience with dozens, hundreds, thousands, or even millions of other people on social media. We are in an age when the message, audience, and means of communication are readily at hand.

Even in the age of social media, news outlets and other mainstream mass media remain important. Experts underscore the importance of social movements capturing the attention of these "people in charge" when trying to nurture widespread change in beliefs, attitudes, and behaviors. In the case of mental health, the people in charge could be lawmakers, police, medical providers, insurance companies, or another target whose decision-making affects larger communities. By keeping the target in mind, advocacy messages on social media can be better tailored to be persuasive, just as any advertiser would do when crafting commercials for a 20-year-old man versus a 60-year-old woman.

To illustrate, political pundits often make controversial remarks on the evening news, expressing anger and prejudice, calling for anti-social behavior from followers. Opponents take to social media, calling for the pundit to apologize, but he stands firm. That is, until the opponents figure out that the offensive pundit should not be the target of persuasive appeals. Instead, they boycott "the people in charge," the corporations funding the pundit's television show through paid advertisements. Advertisers begin dropping simply to avoid the association with controversy. The corporate news channel demands the pundit apologize or go on extended vacation.

Mental health advocates often ask others to "walk a mile" in the shoes of a person who experiences depression, anxiety, schizophrenia, or other conditions. Advocates should do the same for the people they are attempting to persuade. For example, Rachel Jenkins (2013) aptly points out how lawmakers are often voted into office because of issues such as the economy, unemployment, and crime. An advocate who attempts to persuade lawmakers about mental health reform, then, might frame appeals in economic terms: By investing in mental health, lawmakers can save the state economy money by avoiding employee absences.

Another important component of protest is crowd size. The number of people who are involved in the protest can (a) illustrate the significance of the issue and (b) increase attention. In social media, this means employing hashtags, "the digital analogues of hand-held signs at street protests" (Freelon et al., 2018, p. 994). Hashtags permit people to find (and join) the conversation on social media. They also generate increased attention by placing the issue atop the issues "Trending" on Twitter (and other platforms).

Social media platforms—Twitter, Facebook, others—use algorithms to determine which topics are generating intense interest (i.e., going viral). Indeed, business models of social media platforms prefer spikes in communication rather than sustained public interest. Poell and van Dijck (2018, p. 11) describe this as both a "blessing and a curse" for activists: They can reach new and massive audiences, but their messages can quickly fade from public attention as another wave of topics trends.

For all their strengths, social media protests have weaknesses. The nature of social media—where anyone can comment, often anonymously—means mental health protests can become unorganized and even backfire. Protest requires leadership, even when the initiative is informal.

Mental health advocates can draw guidance from organizers of political movements on social media, including Arab Spring and Occupy (for a discussion, see Poell & van Dijck, 2018). The movements functioned from the "bottom up," emerging organically among people with shared desires rather than being dictated by formal organizations. Nonetheless, the movements had leadership. Through social media, leaders helped frame the protest, communicated protest information such as dates and locations, and connected diverse people/organizations who shared interest in the cause. Such organizers are "connective leaders," who are focused on "inviting, connecting, steering, and stimulating, rather than directing, commanding, and proclaiming" (Poell & van Dijck, 2018, p. 4).

Conclusion

The use of news and social media for mental health-related protest remains an underexplored area of research. Nonetheless, mental health advocates can draw insight other fields, including political protest, to develop best practices for media-based protest. Social media has afforded people the power to bypass traditional media outlets, affording the opportunity to present information contrary to established narratives, encourage other people to participate in protests, and inspire additional confidence in the likelihood of protests succeeding (e.g., Tufekci & Wilson, 2012).

While mental health communication and protests in Tahrir Square, or Ferguson, or elsewhere differ dramatically in circumstances, motivations, and outcomes, there are commonalities that mental health advocates can draw upon to persuade people to destigmatize mental illness. First is the revision of the prevailing narrative. Advocates can directly challenge traditional news stories about mental illness through comments beneath stories, social media posts, YouTube videos and other means. Second, social media can be used as a tool to organize, motivate, and inform advocates about the logistics of protest. Online communities form around issues, including mental health, so a Facebook group could schedule times to gather on the steps of the Legislature to demand healthcare parity. Third, persistence and commitment are important (Freelon et al., 2018). As the old saying goes, "The squeaky wheel gets the grease." By persistently calling for change, advocates can pester the people in charge enough to elicit change.

References

Associated Press. (2007). Huckabee says joke was not about suicide. *CBS News*. https://www.cbsnews.com/news/huckabee-says-joke-was-not-about-suicide/

Auxier, B., & Anderson, M. (2021). Social media use in 2021. Pew Research Center. https://www.pewresearch.org/internet/2021/04/07/social-media-use-in-2021/

Barr, J. (2019). Fox News won't book guest again after 'disgraceful' comments about Greta Thunberg. *The Hollywood Reporter*. https://www.hollywoodreporter.com/tv/tv-news/fox-news-wont-book-michael-knowles-again-disgraceful-comments-greta-thunberg-1242789/

Benbow, A. (2007). Mental illness, stigma, and the media. *Journal of Clinical Psychiatry, 68*(Suppl 2), 31–35.

Betton, V., Borschmann, R., Docherty, M., Coleman, S., Brown, M., & Henderson, C. (2015). The role of social media in reducing stigma and discrimination. *The British Journal of Psychiatry, 206*(6), 443–444.

Bremner, J. (2021). Fox News welcomes back guest it vowed to ban over nasty attack on Greta Thunberg. Independent. https://www.independent.co.uk/climate-change/news/fox-news-guest-greta-thunberg-b1880429.html

Chiu, A. (2019). A Fox News guest called Greta Thunberg "mentally ill." The network apologized for the "disgraceful" comment. Washington Post. https://www.washingtonpost.com/nation/2019/09/24/fox-news-greta-thunberg-mentally-ill-michael-knowles/

Community Mental Health Association CMHA of Michigan. (2022). Walk a Mile Rally. https://cmham.org/education-events/walk-a-mile-rally/

Corrigan, P., & Gelb, B. (2006). Three programs that use mass approaches to challenge the stigma of mental illness. *Psychiatric Services, 57*(3), 393–398.

Ettman, C. K., Abdalla, S. M., Cohen, G. H., Sampson, L., Vivier, P. M., & Galea, S. (2020). Prevalence of depression symptoms in US adults before and during the COVID-19 pandemic. JAMA Network Open, *3*(9), e2019686–e2019686.

Freelon, D., McIlwain, C., & Clark, M. (2018). Quantifying the power and consequences of social media protest. New Media & Society, *20*(3), 990–1011.

Jenkins, R. (2013). How to convince politicians that mental health is a priority. *World Psychiatry, 12*(3), 266.

Kessler, R. C., Amminger, G. P., Aguilar-Gaxiola, S., Alonso, J., Lee, S., & Ustun, T. B. (2007). Age of onset of mental disorders: A review of recent literature. *Current Opinion in Psychiatry, 20*(4), 359.

Kezwer, G. (2000, February 8). Candy killed after complaints from mentally disabled Americans. Canadian Medical Association Journal. https://www.cmaj.ca/content/162/3/400.2

Loveridge, M. (2021). Locals rally to urge Bozeman Health to add inpatient psychiatric health care. Bozeman Daily Chronicle. https://www.bozemandailychronicle.com/news/health/locals-rally-to-urge-bozeman-health-to-add-inpatient-psychiatric-health-care/article_b7f2f264-7b12-57ed-ac44-fb15af401491.html

Mukadam, N., & Livingston, G. (2012). Reducing the stigma associated with dementia: Approaches and goals. *Aging Health, 8*(4), 377–386.

Ostrove, J. (2021). WVU students hold mental health protest following student's suicide. WBOY. https://www.wboy.com/news/local/monongalia-and-preston/wvu-students-hold-mental-health-protest-following-students-suicide/

Penn, D. L., & Couture, S. M. (2002). Strategies for reducing stigma toward persons with mental illness. *World Psychiatry, 1*(1), 20.

Poell, T., & van Dijck, J. (2018). Social media and new protest movements. In J. Burgess, A. Marwick, & T. Poell (Eds.), The SAGE Handbook of Social Media. London.

Ritman, A. (2021). Mental health charity confirms talks with ITV over Piers Morgan's Meghan Markle comments. *The Hollywood Reporter.* https://www.hollywoodreporter.com/tv/tv-news/mental-health-charity-confirms-talks-with-itv-over-piers-morgans-meghan-markle-comments-4145575/

Rüsch, N., Angermeyer, M. C., & Corrigan, P. W. (2005). Mental illness stigma: Concepts, consequences, and initiatives to reduce stigma. *European Psychiatry, 20*(8), 529–539.

Scottish Government (2021). Tackling the stigma of addiction. https://www.gov.scot/news/tackling-the-stigma-of-addiction/

Tufekci, Z., & Wilson, C. (2012). Social media and the decision to participate in political protest: Observations from Tahrir Square. *Journal of Communication, 62*(2), 363–379.

10

Educating the Masses: The Potential of Media and Mental Health Literacy

The National Basketball Association launched an initiative to educate players, coaches, and fans about mental health in 2018. The initiative, *Mind Health*, came as professional basketball players and other elite athletes began speaking about the stigma attached to mental illness. Dr. Kensa Gunter, a clinical psychologist based in Atlanta, described the program as holistic one recent afternoon as we talked about mental health and sport.

The initiative, she said, ensures players access to mental health professionals and educates the league about the importance of mental well-being, self-care, and treatment. It also provides resources to the public, featuring stories of elite athletes who are affected by anxiety, depression, and other conditions.

“I think oftentimes experts have ideas on what’s helpful, and we need that,” Gunter said. “But we also need to listen to the people that we’re serving to make sure that what we’re doing is relevant and relatable. We try to listen, provide education, and provide support and resources based on what we hear their needs are.”

The NBA’s mental health program illustrates one way in which the mass media may be used for mental health *education*, which can challenge stigma, normalize conversations about mental health, and improve mental health literacy. This chapter describes research and recommends strategies that anyone—organizations, advocates—can adopt to educate others about mental health.

First, the chapter describes educational efforts targeting mental health literacy, or people's knowledge concerning symptoms, medication, therapy, and other subjects related to mental illness. Second, the chapter delves into mass media literacy, an indirect approach to challenging stigma that involves teaching the public to be more critical consumers of news, movies, and other mass media fare. Third, the chapter reviews studies in entertainment-education, an approach that infuses educational material in television shows, movies, and other entertainment fare, much like wrapping medicine in a tasty treat. Finally, the chapter presents best practice recommendations based on research-to-date, keeping in mind that the field is developing novel approaches for educating the masses every day. Overall, research suggests education via the mass media can improve people's knowledge concerning the symptoms, causes, and treatments of mental illness, while also challenging stigma.

Mental Health Literacy

When people are literate in a subject, they demonstrate knowledge and understanding concerning the topic. The knowledge can inform subsequent behavior. Researchers coined the term "mental health literacy" to describe people's understanding of the myriad components of mental health (e.g., Jorm, 2012). A person who is literate in mental health can identify symptoms of mental illness, connect symptoms with conditions, practice self-care (through mindfulness, exercise, etc.), and understand when it might be time to seek professional help. In addition, the person can identify the types of help available, at least at a basic level.

Mental health advocates have sought to improve the public's mental health literacy after recognizing the importance of the layperson in healthcare and policy (rather than focusing on, say, medical students and lawmakers). Researchers have tested numerous approaches to educating the public about mental health, engaging people through lectures, face-to-face meetings, videos, brochures, and—the focus here—mass media.

Mental health literacy is an umbrella term. Unpack it, and one can see understand the myriad avenues through which mental health advocates can educate the public. For example, advocates might correct misinformed assumptions about schizophrenia being a "split personality." In a piece called "Probing Question," the public relations team at Penn State University educated website visitors to the difference between schizophrenia and dissociative identity disorder (Haycock, 2010). In one survey, 6 in 10 people believed schizophrenia carried symptoms of a "split personality." The university interviewed Randon Welton, a psychiatry professor, who described the misunderstanding as common and understandable. "It's based on the name," he said. "If you go to the Greek roots of the word—schizein, meaning splitting and phren, meaning mind—you have 'split brain' or 'split mind.' However, the intended reference is to a split between rationality and emotions, not a split within a personality" (para. 3).

In addition to educating the public, mental health advocates might help family members understand what to expect from a loved one who was recently diagnosed with an illness. In this case, they could help families understand what their loved one is going through, what they might expect, and who can help. For example, the Canadian Mental Health Association (2016) provides families recommendations on how they might help after a loved one has been diagnosed with schizophrenia. "Many people say they're not sure how to best help when a loved one experiences a mental illness like schizophrenia," the organization wrote on the *HereToHelp* website. The organization provides families fact sheets, information for advocacy societies, support group calendars, and practical suggestions such as "Listen," "Use empathy, not arguments," "Don't take it personally," and "Take care of yourself, too." *HereToHelp* is a collective of mental health organizations in British Columbia, and its website is designed to help people "find quality information, learn new skills, and connect with key resources."

These scenarios illustrate key considerations mental health advocates must take into account when developing programs to educate others about mental health. First, who is the audience? Second, what is the desired outcome? Third, how will mass media tools be used to implement the pedagogical material? The first scenario targeted people curious about schizophrenia, educating visitors to the Penn State website who might have found the story using search engines (e.g., Google) or by following the university on social media. *HereToHelp*, meanwhile, specifically educated people whose loved ones were diagnosed with schizophrenia. The target audience meant the organization provided different educational material, although the organization employed a comparable (and increasingly common) delivery method of social media and website.

Anthony Jorm, a psychologist in Australia, described literacy as empowerment, noting that it "is not simply a matter of having knowledge . . . Rather it is knowledge that is linked to the possibility of action to benefit one's own mental health or that of others" (2012, p. 231). Jorm describes mental health literacy as understanding how to prevent disorders, recognizing when one is developing, and understanding treatment options. It also involves knowing "first aid," or the ability to help others who are experiencing disorders or crises. Education, then, can target people's knowledge of symptoms so they can avoid delays in seeking help (or in connecting loved ones with help). Initiatives might also seek to improve people's ability to identify sources and types of mental health care. Finally, educational interventions might adopt holistic approaches, helping people understand prevention, diagnosis, and treatment options.

For lessons to work, mental health advocates must identify the audience they are targeting. Educators are likely to experience greater success when they identify the knowledge gaps, biases, and other important characteristics of their target audience. For example, the Opening Minds in Canada program adopted different approaches while working to improve mental health literacy among four target groups: youth, health care providers, workplaces, and media (Stuart et al., 2014). It trained health care providers to better interact with people affected by severe mental illness. In the workplace, it focused on challenging stigma and helping employees (and employers) develop coping strategies. For media producers, Opening Minds developed resources to help journalists identify sources for stories, quickly find facts about mental illness, and see examples of stigma-challenging stories. When advocates identify a target audience, they can better understand needs while also predicting potential pitfalls. To illustrate, the Opening Minds team described the advocate/employer relationship as a courting, one in which the employers "often show initial interest in a partnership, and then interest fades"(p. S17). By identifying potential issues in advance, educators can develop plans to bypass barriers.

As Jorm noted, mental health literacy represents empowerment. Initiatives might also enjoy greater success when the audience is involved in the creation of the message. For example, mental health advocates in Canada worked hand-in-hand with youths to develop and test the effectiveness of a mental health literacy project called MindQuest (Syan et al., 2021). The teens were involved in everything from the information contained in the program to how it was presented. Such a community approach can help messages better resonate with an intended audience.

The mass media afford educators relatively low cost, far-reaching methods by which to teach people about the symptoms, causes, and treatments of mental illness. Educators who are interested in producing high-quality videos can simply use smartphones, thanks to advancements in technology and the relatively low cost. Though limited in effectiveness, web-based educational programs show promise in improving public beliefs, attitudes, and behavior related to mental health (Brijnath et al., 2016).

Bianca Brinjath and colleagues (2016) reviewed research testing the effectiveness of web-based mental health literacy programs. The programs ranged in the topics they addressed, from teaching military families to understand Post Traumatic Stress Disorder to helping parents identify depression symptoms in adolescents. Web-based programs were largely successful when they were structured, interactive, and informed by pedagogy (i.e., good teaching practices). Programs struggled when they simply provided people information in a way that could be seen as condescending or having an ulterior moral lesson. Put simply, people must be engaged in an interactive dialogue and not feel as though they are being lectured.

Media Literacy: Providing People Tools

A growing movement is occurring in which scholars are examining how we can train audiences to be more critical media consumers. Media literacy is defined in different ways. It can involve a person's ability to use technology safely and effectively, an important skill in today's labor force. Media literacy can also focus on a person's critical thinking skills in relation to mass media content. For example, a teenager who is media literate might recognize the fabrication behind a cover model's body, the airbrushing responsible for the 6-pack abs and lack of fat. By understanding the manipulation, the teenager could be better equipped to avoid comparing their own body to the image. Livingstone (2004) describes media literacy as a four-stage process involving "the ability to access, analyze, evaluate, and create messages in a variety of forms" (p. 3).

To illustrate, my colleague Dr. Kim Bissell visited local schools and taught adolescents to identify the "thin ideal" in mass media content. She helped girls dissect advertisements for beauty products and fashion magazines, identifying how the photographs of super models and pop singers were digitally altered to make them appear thinner. The goal of the lessons was indirect, in part: By teaching children to be more critical media consumers, they can be empowered to avoid feeling shame over their own appearance. The importance of the lessons is underscored by research that connects media exposure with eating disorders such as bulimia and anorexia. Dr. Bissell's work is in line with the literacy movements in mental health and media, which both involve empowerment and the inclusion of people who are affected. For example, Bergsma (2004) recommends media literacy programs recognize the potential power of youths as influencers. Bergsma writes (p. 154) "helping youth to channel their natural developmental rebellion, their fresh perspective, and their unique energy and creativity toward accomplishing social change, based on youth-identified social concerns . . . should be a primary focus." Media literacy programs may help empower people affected by mental illness, leading to not only prevention but what Bergsma (2004) describes as a sense of community and improved quality of life.

Social Media: Providing Content and Context

Education need not be formal. The ubiquity of social media means typical people can reach millions of people with a few taps of the thumb and a press of the send button. This affords advocates power to educate the public about mental health without serious financial or time commitment. The power should be respected, though, because it also means other people can respond to advocates' posts, at times spreading misinformation or negative emotions.

Through social media, advocates can directly appeal to other users by posting original content or they can share helpful information by responding to other people's content, including news stories, videos, and social media posts.

Social Media: Sharing Original Content

Advocates can create their own content to educate others about mental health and the mass media. For example, a woman named Lauren posts videos on YouTube in which she explains what it is like to live with schizophrenia (Living Well, 2020). Nearly 150,000 people subscribe to her channel, Living Well with Schizophrenia, which means they receive notices every time she posts another video. In May 2020, Lauren posted a 34-minute video titled "Are Schizophrenia Simulations Accurate?" in which she (and home viewers) watched VR simulations of schizophrenia and dissected which aspects were realistic or misleading. The video generated 2.3 million views and elicited more than 11,000 comments in 18 months. Viewers praised the lesson. One commenter wrote, "I can't imagine what schizophrenic people go through." Another wrote, "As a mental health therapist, I can honestly say that your channel has helped me learn more about Schizophrenic Disorder Spectrum than any textbook ever has, Lauren."

The *Living Well with Schizophrenia* channel represents only one approach. Mental health advocates can also share helpful self-care information with followers. For example, the National Alliance on Mental Illness uses the social media platform Twitter to reach nearly 176,000 followers. Each post stands the chance of reaching even more people, as Twitter users can share the posts with their own account followers. For example, one afternoon in December 2021, @ NAMICommunicate shared posts about grief during the holidays (retweeted 30 times, liked by 42 people), mental health tips for men in college (retweeted 9 times, liked 18 times), and signs that mental health professionals might be experiencing burnout (retweeted 71 times, liked 134 times).

Perhaps the greatest challenge for advocates who post their own content is competing against the sheer amount of information online. Advocates must be methodical and persistent, adopting strategies to ensure people pay attention and digest the information they are sharing. Research is lacking when it comes to mental health and educational interventions on social media. Still, advocates can borrow strategies from other fields (such as marketing) to develop successful techniques for educating others.

First, advocates should post regularly on blogs, social media accounts, and other platforms to engage and maintain an audience. Second, advocates should mind emotions. Research suggests news stories, social media posts, and other online content stands the greatest chance of "going viral" when it elicits emotional reactions (e.g., Berger & Milkman, 2013). Two powerful emotions are anger and inspiration. Anger is potentially dangerous because it could nurture negative comments and reactions, devolving an otherwise educational interaction. Hope appears to be a better approach to helping people understand causes, consequences, and treatments of mental illness, and the people who are affected. For example, a mother posted a photograph on Facebook of a college football player choosing to sit beside her son in the school cafeteria (Hauser, 2016). The child, who has autism, had been sitting alone because schoolmates did not understand him. The post went viral, generating empathy and presumably a desire to learn what people experience when they have autism. Christopher A. Bail, a researcher at Duke University, illustrated the importance of emotional engagement while studying viral Facebook posts about Autism Spectrum Disorder (Bail, 2016). A number of factors predict the likelihood of posts going viral; indeed, the strongest predictors were an advocacy organization's use of audiovisuals and the sheer size of their fanbase. An advocacy organization also engaged more Facebook users when a post conveyed positive emotional language.

Providing Context, Correcting Misinformation

Mental health advocates can also use social media to supplement existing stories, posts, and other online content about mental health. For example, Anna Rae Gwarjanski examined how journalists for traditional news publications (*The New York Times, Washington Post*) and online news publications (*Buzzfeed, The Huffington Post*) covered schizophrenia. After analyzing 558 stories, she found that the so-called digital news outlets covered a breadth of subjects, featuring first-person essays about schizophrenia, articles about innovations in healthcare, and other educational material. Traditional outlets, though, focused on murder and mayhem. During this period, it seemed these influential journalists covered schizophrenia only when it came up during the criminal trials of mass shooters. Comments accompanying the stories were no better. Among other discriminatory appeals, comments called for the criminal justice system to "lock up" anyone with mental illness and "throw away the key."

People are increasingly getting news through online sources, including websites and social media, where readers can often leave comments. Comment sections can be full of vitriol, but they are also read. Mental health advocates can share helpful information beneath news stories and social media posts, providing additional context or building off an original post. In the case of the shooting, mental health advocates might anticipate the response beneath articles on mainstream websites such as *The New York Times*, *CNN*, or *Fox News*. Through collective action, advocates can flood the comment sections with educational and helpful information, essentially drowning out the "throw away the key" style comments. As noted in Chapter 2, journalists and other mass communicators often perpetuate stereotypes about mental illness. Social media affords advocates an opportunity to respond without being dependent upon the journalist.

Entertainment-Education

In addition to direct appeals, health educators are demonstrating the value of wrapping educational information in entertainment. Health educators borrowed a technique from advertisers—product placement—which involves selling brands by planting advertisements in television shows, films, and even press conferences. Instead of soda pop, health educators worked with screenwriters to communicate health-related information into storylines. There is good reason to adopt such an approach. Medical shows are among the most watched programs in the United

States, with programs such as *Grey's Anatomy* reaching millions of viewers each week. Could inserting educational information into the plotlines teach viewers healthy beliefs and behavior?

The idea builds off the phenomenon of narrative persuasion, which suggests that people drop their mental defenses and become wrapped up in dramatic television shows and movies, identifying with characters and the travails they encounter as the stories unfold. People can be persuaded and educated by information they encounter while focused on the twists and turns of the narrative; they could walk away smarter and not even realize they had been taught. Ritterfield and Jin (206, p. 248) described this entertainment-education approach as "the process of designing and implementing a media message in order to increase knowledge about an educational issue, create favorable attitudes toward socially desirable targets, shift social norms and change behaviors."

In 1996, the Australian director Michael Rymer released the award-winning film "Angel Baby," which tells the story of two people with schizophrenia who "meet during therapy and fall passionately in love. Ahead of them lies the inevitable road to disaster – one they share to the end" (IMDB, 2022). Ritterfield and Jin (2006) wanted to know whether the film, which contained factual and empathetic information about schizophrenia, could improve viewers' knowledge and attitudes about schizophrenia. To do so, the researchers had university students complete a questionnaire about schizophrenia and watch the movie. In addition, the researchers packaged the movie with a short educational message conveyed by a mental health professional or person affected by schizophrenia. "I hope this film has shown you that people with mental disorders are not just the sum of their disorders," an actor stated in the video. "Just like Kate and Harry, they all have talents, skills, and individual personalities." Later, the actor added, "Because the media, whether films, television or the news, often associate mental illness with violent behavior, people tend to think that those who have a psychiatric disability are dangerous. But as you could see in the film, they are far more likely to be frightened than to frighten others" (p. 264). In the end, the entertainment-education approach worked. Viewers were more knowledgeable about schizophrenia after the experience. In addition, after the film, 33% endorsed a stereotype associating schizophrenia with violent behavior. Before the viewing, 99% of the students had agreed with the stereotype.

Leopoldo J. Cabassa and colleagues (2015) targeted depression stigma among Latino adults using *fotonovelas*, "popular health education tools that use posed photographs, captions, and soap opera narratives to engage audiences and raise awareness about health or social issues" (p. 313). The research team developed a bilingual fotonovela called "Secret Feelings," which combined education and vicarious contact with depressed characters. Researchers visited adult night schools in Los Angeles, where they asked students to complete questionnaires that measured their knowledge and attitudes about depression. Afterward, the students read either a depression brochure or the fotonovela, and later completed the knowledge and attitude questionnaire a second time. The experiment found mixed results. The fotonovela appeared no better than the standard brochure at challenging stigma and improving knowledge about depression. However, students who read the fotonovela did report greater knowledge concerning depression treatment.

"Secret Feelings" provided the content for another experiment with entertainment-education, this time in San Francisco. Maria Y. Hernandez and Kurt C. Organista (2013) had immigrant Latina women read the fotonovela and then compared their knowledge and attitudes about depression to women who did not read it. Compared to the control group, women who read the fotonovela showed greater knowledge concerning depression, greater self-efficacy regarding treatment, and reduced stigma toward anti-depressant medication.

Overall, the results of these mental health-related studies are in line with entertainment-education effects from other health fields. A review of 22 studies by Fuyuan Shen and Jiangxue Han (2014) determined that entertainment education is effective at improving knowledge, but less effective when it comes to altering attitudes and behavior.

Conclusion

Overall, we can draw a number of best-practice recommendations for challenging stigma through education via mass media. Granted, a number of factors might affect the ability of mass media to alter stereotypes, prejudice, and discrimination through education. Still, there are basic tenets mental health advocates might take into account. These include:

Lessons should be engaging (and preferably not even feel like a lesson). Advocates should remember they are vying for an audience whose attention is bombarded by information. You could preach to the choir, teaching mental health advocates. However, the most effective lessons will reach larger audiences who might not be invested or interested in the subject at first glance.

Lessons should focus on the accurate and helpful. De-bunking stereotypes can certainly be helpful. However, by repeating stereotypes (such as the false association between violence and schizophrenia), you risk planting a seed in the minds of audience members who otherwise might not be familiar with the problematic belief. A better approach involves focusing on positive messages when educating the public about mental health.

Lessons should be non-confrontational. It would be an understatement to describe the world of social media as emotional. Comments beneath videos, news stories, and personal posts can be downright toxic. Avoid the muck. For example, when journalists blame mental illness for a mass shooting, leaving out context, you can close the gap in the comment section beneath the story by providing facts. Provide evidence to contradict inaccurate information and avoid back-and-forth arguments with people whose opinions probably cannot be altered. Mental health advocates can also reach out to journalists through email, social media, or direct messages. Again, educate rather than correct. A simple email could say "John, a lot of journalists who are covering this story are forgetting this important context. I thought you might be interested . . . "

Lessons should nurture dialogue. The toxic combination of social media and politics has nurtured an environment in which dialogue seems nonexistent at times. Through dialogue, we can engage other people and communicate opinions/facts while respecting the other party's opinion. When using social media to educate others about mental illness, use the opportunity to nurture dialogue. An organization, for example, could include an invitation to a livestream in which experts will discuss a controversy. A person affected by mental illness can invite others to ask questions.

Finally, **lessons should consider the audience.** Who are you targeting? Imagine the daily lives of your audience. What would be helpful? It is easy to be reactive rather than proactive. In other words, mental health advocates can focus educational efforts on challenging stigma and responding to controversies. Mental health education can also be communicated through tips that will help people while they navigate the demands of work, parenting, morning commutes, and other tasks that dominate their time. For example, a simple statement can elicit positive outcomes and quickly spread by generating "likes" and sharing on social media: "Did you know? Tell someone you know one positive thing today. It can help your mental health – and theirs!"

References

Bail, C. A. (2016). Emotional feedback and the viral spread of social media messages about autism spectrum disorders. *American Journal of Public Health, 106*(7), 1173–1180.

Berger, J., & Milkman, K. L. (2013). Emotion and virality: What makes online content go viral?. *NIM Marketing Intelligence Review, 5*(1), 18–23.

Brijnath, B., Protheroe, J., Mahtani, K. R., & Antoniades, J. (2016). Do web-based mental health literacy interventions improve the mental health literacy of adult consumers? Results from a systematic review. *Journal of Medical Internet Research, 18*(6), e5463.

Cabassa, L. J., Oh, H., Humensky, J. L., Unger, J. B., Molina, G. B., & Baron, M. (2015). Comparing the impact on Latinos of a depression brochure and an entertainment-education depression fotonovela. *Psychiatric Services, 66*(3), 313–316.

Canadian Mental Health Association. (2016). Someone I love has been diagnosed with schizophrenia. How can I help? *HereToHelp.* https://www.heretohelp.bc.ca/q-and-a/someone-i-love-has-been-diagnosed-with-schizophrenia

Hauser, C. (2016). Photo of F.S.U. football star sitting with boy eating alone at school charms internet. *The New York Times.* https://www.nytimes.com/2016/09/02/us/photo-of-fsu-football-star-sitting-with-boy-eating-alone-at-florida-school-charms-internet.html

Haycock, D. (2010). Probing question: How do schizophrenia and DID differ? Penn State University. https://www.psu.edu/news/research/story/probing-question-how-do-schizophrenia-and-did-differ/

Hernandez, M. Y., & Organista, K. C. (2013). Entertainment–education? A fotonovela? A new strategy to improve depression literacy and help-seeking behaviors in at-risk immigrant Latinas. *American Journal of Community Psychology, 52*(3), 224–235.

Living Well with Schizophrenia (2020). Are schizophrenia simulations accurate? https://www.youtube.com/watch?v=60n7ZP3Cj-4

Livingstone, S. (2004). What is media literacy?. *Intermedia, 32*(3), 18–20.

Ritterfeld, U., & Jin, S. A. (2006). Addressing media stigma for people experiencing mental illness using an entertainment-education strategy. *Journal of Health Psychology, 11*(2), 247–267.

Shen, F., & Han, J. (2014). Effectiveness of entertainment education in communicating health information: A systematic review. *Asian Journal of Communication, 24*(6), 605–616.

11

Walk in My Digital Shoes: Using Games & VR to Nurture Empathy

Ominous music plays as a news camera pans over traffic in the big city. Barbara Walters, the famed news anchor, appears on screen. She sits in an armchair in a news studio, her hands clasped on her lap. She looks concerned.

"We've all heard stories of people saying they were driven nearly crazy by voices in their head," she says, "distracting them, commanding them to hurt themselves, occasionally to hurt others. But now, for the first time, you can actually experience for a few moments what these people live with as they struggle with the illness known as . . . schizophrenia."

It's 20/20 Friday, a national news program on ABC in the United States. Walters and her correspondent, Dr. Timothy Johnson, are there to share news "of an amazing futuristic breakthrough that puts you inside a tortured mind." The program later cuts to Johnson standing inside a doctor's office, anatomy posters and medical instruments hanging on the wall behind him. Now, he tells viewers, there is a way for experts to "truly get in the mind of a schizophrenic."

Specifically, Johnson is informing viewers about new virtual reality equipment developed by Janssen Pharmaceuticals. The technology, a combination of goggles and headphones, permits users to digitally adopt the perspective of a person who experiences auditory and visual hallucinations, symptoms of schizophrenia. Johnson first sets the stage for the home viewer, describing voices people hear all the time, especially at night. "All the voices are evil intonations urging destruction and harm," he says, as the horror music continues.

Johnson dons the equipment himself, and the VR simulation begins. Home viewers receive a peek of the experience, watching as the VR user stands in a psychiatrist's office. Classical music plays. The lights are dimmed. A physician sits behind a desk and asks, "Have you been seeing anything unusual?" Although the user's avatar does not respond verbally, the computer animation suggests that yes, he has seen something unusual: a third eye growing out of the doctor's forehead. Voices whisper. The physician turns into the devil, hellfire glowing behind him.

Returning to home viewers, Johnson apparently wants to confirm the validity of the experience, so he hands the VR equipment to a man who experienced symptoms of schizophrenia in real life. As the camera rolls, the man sweats and breathes heavily. He finally hands off the equipment and staggers away, saying "I'm sorry guys."

The news broadcast, originally aired in 2008, is problematic in many ways. The show uses the term "schizophrenics," instead of people-first language. It reinforces stereotypes when Walters stresses the potential of people harming others because of schizophrenia. She also uses the label "these people," performing the stigmatizing action of separating society into "us" and "them." Finally, the program ventures into ethically questionable territory by using VR on a person with a history of auditory and visual hallucinations. Despite the problems, the news broadcast highlights a growing area in stigma research. Parents, teachers, religious leaders, and others have long encouraged people to "walk a mile in the shoes" of others. Technological innovation is permitting people to do so digitally, for better and worse.

Perspective Taking: An Overview

Researchers have a couple of names for the action of adopting another person's viewpoint. In psychology, researchers call the behavior "perspective-taking," used here because it is the original term. Researchers in mass communication describe the phenomenon as "identification." Regardless of terminology, the behavior involves adopting the viewpoint of another person and attempting to imagine the world through their perspective.

Social psychologists have found that the simple act can challenge stigma related to race, age, mental illness, and other marginalized conditions. It can nurture empathy toward people and social groups, reduce stereotypical thinking, and increase the mental overlap between oneself and other people. The mass media are especially effective in providing environments for perspective taking, as one might expect, because producers understand that immersive stories keep eyes glued to the television, news site, or video game, and audiences translate into money. As described later, a growing movement of game designers, journalists, and researchers are motivated less by financial gain and more by greater social good. Through their work, we are starting to understand the power of interactive media in nurturing empathy and prosocial behavior through perspective-taking with media characters.

This chapter focuses on two promising and evolving mediums—video games and virtual reality. Interventions need not use high-tech gadgets to achieve positive results. For example, Martinez and colleagues (2018) had participants use a low fidelity approach by simply asking them to imagine themselves in the shoes of another person. People might avoid taking or continuing antidepressants because of stigma, so the researchers wanted to develop an efficient method for mitigating negative attitudes toward the use of antidepressants. The research team asked college students to watch videos in which people discussed their experiences with depression. Next, students were asked to "Imagine you are suffering from depression. Please write a paragraph describing an average day in your life. Also consider how your life could change with antidepressants." The task appeared to work, as the students expressed less stigmatizing attitudes toward taking anti-depressants than did people in a control condition.

Similarly, Mann and Himelein (2008) tested a simple approach by asking college students to write poetry from the point of view of someone affected by schizophrenia or bipolar disorder. Participants first watched a 30-minute video in which three young adults—including two college students—discussed their experiences with mental illness. The documentaries also included interviews with family and friends. Before the intervention, the research team measured participants' attitudes toward people with schizophrenia and depression. They measured the same attitudes after the exercise. Through three studies, the intervention worked: Participants' attitudes improved.

In other studies, people "experience" schizophrenia by hearing auditory hallucinations via headphones (Ando et al., 2011). This approach was illustrated by CNN anchor Anderson Cooper in 2014, when he tried to understand what it is like to live with schizophrenia by using a sound simulator (CNN, 2014). Wearing headphones, Cooper sat at a desk and tried to recall words, numbers, and the names of the last four presidents. The task was complicated by a woman's voice coming through the headphones, not frightening or menacing, but interfering with Cooper's—and the home viewers'—focus. "It's hard because sometimes voices are whispering, sometimes they're aggressive, and sometimes they're kind of comforting," he says. "With people talking to you all the time, it's hard." The voices seemingly respond by saying, "Don't worry, it will be OK." Cooper then attempts to follow instructions for making an oragami boat. A voice suddenly shouts "Shut up!" and an exasperated Cooper says, "I really want to talk back to the voices now, so." He finally quits and says, "I can't do this." Walking down the street later, Cooper tells home viewers that "It's really eye opening because it shows you what other people must be going through who deal with this on a regular basis."

When people find themselves enthralled in narratives, they become less likely to challenge the information they encounter. For example, Ma and Nan (2018) examined college students' attitudes toward the mentally ill after they read one of three stories—a first-person narrative, a third-person narrative, or a just-the-facts article about schizophrenia. The narratives followed a character named Lucy, describing her professional achievements, her experiences with mental illnesses, and her recovery after seeking help. "I guess the moment I started recovering was when I asked for help in coping with schizophrenia," she says. The narrative elicited more positive attitudes toward mental illness when compared to the control condition, and evidence suggested that depressed counterarguing explained the effect.

Overall, perspective-taking can achieve results no matter the medium. From virtual reality to simple imagination exercises, the experience of adopting another person's viewpoint appears to nurture empathy and increase self-other overlap.

Perspective-Taking Via Media

The mass media provide numerous ways to adopt the viewpoint of another person. While watching movies, people can become transported into the narrative, adopting attitudes in line with the main characters (Green & Brock, 2000). People can identify with the protagonist of a novel, adopting (for at least a minute) the hero's viewpoint as she navigates dangerous and dilemmas. Listeners can even disappear into a song, considering the world from the viewpoint of the lyricist. The act does not require much more than an active imagination and willingness to see the world through another person's eyes. Nonetheless, imagination may no longer be required because of technological advancements in virtual reality and video games.

Virtual Reality

Once relegated to science fiction, virtual reality is becoming more common in modern life. The technology, which uses animation, sound, and movement to mimic reality, has become better and cheaper, making it more accessible to the typical person. To illustrate, *The New York Times* launched an app with which smartphone users could "experience" three-dimensional stories about everything from sports to warfare. Users could watch an Olympic skater pirouette behind a co-worker's desk, or survey the damage of war-torn Syria. In the research world, scientists have sought to understand whether virtual reality could elicit prosocial outcomes.

If typewritten notes and tape recordings could challenge prejudice, might VR represent perspective-taking on overdrive? Traditional media such as radio and television showed promise while triggering one or two senses. Could virtual reality do more, given its engagement with sound, sight, touch, and—at times—even smell? The answer is yes. And no.

As with parasocial contact (see Chapter 7), the quality of an interaction is incredibly important in determining whether an experience will challenge stigma. Perspective taking likely works best when the experience highlights the humanity of the people involved. In other words, rather than focusing on symptoms of illness, perspective-taking (VR or otherwise) appears to work best when it highlights shared human experience. For example, Yuen and Mak (2021) adopted a "person-centered approach"(p. 2) when conducting an experiment with VR and mental illness stigma. In Hong Kong, Yuen and Mak (2021) had university students use virtual reality to navigate a day in the life of a person with anxiety and depression. The researchers tested two types of VR: an animated version in which users adopted an avatar to engage the immersive storyline, or a version in which participants heard a narrator read the story.

In the simulation, users adopted the perspective of a protagonist named Yan who works in an office and spends time sitting on the sofa at home, conversing with her uncle. Yan experiences stigma and pressure from work and family, as well as self-targeted comments such as "I can do nothing well!" A third group of students served as a control group, watching a video about immersive virtual reality. Going into the study, the students' attitudes concerning mental health appeared comparable. However, students who used the virtual reality headset subsequently expressed less stigmatizing attitudes than their peers in the control group, and the effect lingered one week later when researchers checked back with the students.

Virtual reality has been described as the "ultimate empathy machine" because of its ability to immerse users in the perspective of another person. Given the high praise, Herrera and colleagues (2018) sought to determine whether perspective-taking via immersive virtual environments would elicit comparable (if not better) effects than the traditional approach in which people are asked to imagine themselves in another person's shoes. While both approaches nurtured empathy, the research team discovered that people who used the VR equipment stood greater likelihood of signing a petition to benefit the stigmatized group (in this case, homeless people).

The positive results can be long-lasting. Herrera's team sent participants follow-up surveys two, four, and eight weeks after the virtual reality session in which they adopted the perspective of a homeless person. The researchers found lingering results: Participants who walked a digital mile expressed more positive attitudes toward the homeless even two weeks after the session.

The effectiveness of virtual reality and other mediated perspective taking may lie in the senses. Virtual reality can engage the user's hearing, sight, touch, and even smell, while traditional perspective-taking tasks depend on the person's imagination (and our abilities to envision hypothetical scenarios certainly differ). Based on existing evidence, Sara Ventura and colleagues (2020) concluded that "VR tasks may be more effective at improving attitudes toward specific social targets and motivating prosocial behavior compared with traditional interventions adopted so far," (p. 8). The researchers described two concepts—presence and embodiment—as important factors in the ability of VR to elicit empathy. Presence captures "the projection of the self into the experience of another person," while embodiment takes the experience a step further to represent "being present inside someone else's body" (p. 7). VR provides the "ability to modify the perception of the body's boundaries, giving the illusion of being another person" (p. 7).

Video Games

Video games have long gotten a bad reputation as parents, politicians, pundits, and even researchers described negative outcomes associated with gaming. Granted, in certain contexts, video games can become addicting, feed aggression, and displace time that could be spent doing more productive things like exercising. Still, video games can have positive effects on individuals and society. Indeed, in recent years, the video game industry has witnessed the rise of the so-called serious game, a broad genre in which players navigate social, political, and other important issues—including mental illness.

To illustrate, gamers can attempt to collect water while dodging murderous gang members in *Darfur is Dying*, learning about the lives of refugees trapped by violence (Games for Change, 2022a). They can try to live on minimum wage in *Spent*, weighing difficult decisions to avoid becoming homeless because of lost jobs, broken down cars, medical bills, and other financial problems (Urban Ministries of Durham, 2022). They can try to survive harsh working conditions in *Sweatshop*, learning about the manipulation and abuse of workers who are often children (Games for Change, 2022b). Serious games, produced by everyone from newsrooms to homeless shelters, humanize social issues by teaching gamers in a novel and engaging way. Researchers are beginning to quantify the potential of the games. For example, one research team had young adults play an interactive computer game in which users adopted the perspective of an immigrant illegally crossing the U.S./Mexico border. Gamers made choices concerning the route—mountain or desert or city—and means by which they would attempt to cross the border. Along the way, they encountered information about the dangers faced by undocumented immigrants. People who spent time with the game expressed more support for governmental policies that would benefit undocumented immigrants.

Although research is scant, evidence suggests serious and other video games can also help destigmatize mental illness. Ferchaud and colleagues (2020) tested whether people would endorse fewer stereotypes and desire less social distance after playing a video game in which the main character has mental illness. Specifically, gamers played 45 minutes of *Hellblade: Senua's Sacrifice*, a game in which players adopt the role of Senua as she battles for the soul of her partner. Senua experiences psychosis during the narrative, including auditory hallucinations that the game designers scripted in partnership with mental health experts and a neuroscientist. The researchers hypothesized that the interactive nature of the video game would lead players to become transported into the storyline, reducing stereotypes about mental illness and translating into less desire for social distance from people with mental illness in the real world. The research team had a second group of participants watch other people play the game, enabling a test of their hypothesis concerning the interactive nature of the gameplay. The results were promising. Although stereotypes were not significantly affected, gamers reported less desire for social distance from people with mental illness.

Schlote and Major (2021) sought to understand how prosocial video games might serve as learning devices for mental health. The scholars found four successful video games in which (a) a main character experienced mental illness and (b) the creative team worked alongside mental health experts or consumers in the development process. In addition to *Hellblade* (2017), games included *Debris* (2017), *Please Knock On My Door* (2017), and *Sea Hero Quest* (2016). The games represent diverse genres, from mythical quest to puzzle solving. Mental health issues appeared explicitly, as game designers informed players at the beginning of the characters' mental illness in all but one. Although the authors commended the video games for incorporating mental health themes into the storylines, they described their usefulness for educating the public as limited.

Considerations: Negative Outcomes

Galinsky and colleagues (2005, p. 109) described perspective-taking as "an engine of social harmony," that "can also reveal a dark side, one full of ironic consequences." That dark side can emerge in media content, and mental health advocates should keep in mind the power of stereotype confirmation. In other words, when an individual adopts the perspective of another person and the experience simply reinforces stereotypes, the individual will likely leave the experience with comparable—or even worse—attitudes than before. Perspective-taking can be a double-edged sword, actually increasing stereotypes when the experience confirms an individual's existing (and misguided) notions about mental health. For example, Shapiro and Rotter (2016) found almost all of the 96 highest-selling video games between 2011 and 2013 included at least one character with mental illness, and it was often in relation to violence. If a person "walks a mile" in the shoes of one of these characters and witnesses (or perpetuates) virtual violence, they will probably conclude the experience thinking (a) people with mental illness are violent and (b) desiring social distance from people with mental illness.

Virtual reality and video games are promising areas for mental health advocacy, and technology is improving such that even novices can design simple interactive games. Still, advocates should exercise caution. While perspective-taking appears simple on its face, it is a complex phenomenon in which the content of the conjured image can shift whether the outcome is pro- or anti-social. Indeed, research suggests stereotype-confirming perspective-taking can nurture stereotypical thinking (Skorinko & Sinclair, 2013). When outgroup members confirm existing stereotypes, Skorinko and Sinclair write (p. 17), perspective taking can feed into additional stereotypical thinking, "presumably because perspective takers use the salient stereotypic information as a theory with which to generate the thoughts and feelings of the target." Herrera et al. (2018) described the positive outcomes of perspective taking as "contextually bound," noting the potential for immersive virtual experiences to backfire and elicit anti-social effects.

Kalyanaraman and colleagues (2010) encountered such results when they tested a virtual reality simulation about schizophrenia. In one condition, participants entered the perspective of John, a person with schizophrenia, as he bought medication for the disorder. While John walks through the pharmacy, he notices nearby people step away, he hears voices, and he sees the medication turn to poison. The researchers wondered whether people would feel greater empathy toward John—and other people with schizophrenia—after the VR experience. Instead, the intervention partially backfired. People expressed more empathy, but they also reported increased desire to maintain social distance from people like John. Still, the experiment found potential for VR, as users reported more empathy (but not an increased desire for social distance) after also reading an empathy prompt (e.g., "try and really put yourself in that person's place . . . "). The researchers note (p. 441) that presumably participants "could use the information from the empathy manipulation to regulate the responses that may have stemmed as a result of exposure to the virtual simulation."

An explanation for the undesirable outcome can be found in stereotype confirmation. The general public often endorses stereotypes in which schizophrenia is associated with unpredictable and violent behavior. Such stereotypes are simply validated when people hear virtual voices suggesting they should shoot themselves (Ando et al., 2011) or see a three-eyed man leaning toward them and asking "What's wrong with you?" The experience communicates to VR users that yes, they should feel bad for people with schizophrenia, and yes, they should keep their distance because there is no telling what the person might do.

Similar results emerged when Na and Chasteen (2016) tested the efficacy of imagined contact and perspective-taking in challenging stigma. In laboratory and community settings, the researchers found imagined contact to be more effective in reducing stigma. In some instances, the perspective-taking seemed to nurture stereotypic thinking. The researchers offered two possible explanations, stereotype confirmation and self-esteem threat. "Perhaps imagining what it is like to be depressed makes people feel more vulnerable to that possibility, resulting in feelings of discomfort," the researchers wrote (p. 272).

In another example, Brown (2020) compared two potential mass media interventions—video contact and perspective-taking via audio/video simulation. Participants watched *Living with Schizophrenia,* a 16-minute video in which three people with schizophrenia described their symptoms, challenges, treatment, and accomplishments. A second group watched *Mindstorm*, the audio/visual simulation developed by Janssen Pharmaceuticals. Echoing other studies, participants expressed less stigmatizing attitudes related to dangerousness, negative emotions, and desired social distance after the video. However, the simulation seemed ineffective, leading Brown to conclude that "At present, audio/visual simulations do not appear promising in significantly lowering stigma among the general population" (p. 476). However, the problem likely lay in the content of the simulation, rather than the experience itself.

Conclusion

Perspective-taking is an effective method for challenging the stigma attached to mental illness. The mass media are extremely effective at immersing audiences in the lives of characters, and research suggests that walking a mile in the shoes of a character can reduce stereotypical thinking—when done right. Indeed, there is a dark side to perspective-taking in which the act can nurture stereotypes by simply confirming a person's misguided beliefs about what it means to live with mental illness. Therefore, advocates should exercise caution and pilot test material to determine whether narratives, games, VR experiences, and other immersive content elicit the anticipated results.

Judging by prior research, advocates should ensure storylines largely challenge rather than confirm stereotypes. The word "largely" is used because advocates should also ensure the person represents (for the audience) the broader group of people with depression, or schizophrenia, or bipolar disorder. Otherwise, audiences could dismiss the character as an outlier and non-representative of the social group. The greatest art captures shared human experience. So, too, should perspective-taking tasks. By accentuating the humanity of people with mental illness, advocates can enhance empathy and the self/other overlap, challenging stigma.

Philosophers—from Buddhist monks to modern parents—have long encouraged people to imagine the world from the perspective of another person. Indeed, the Vietnamese monk Thich Nhat Hanh recommends we remember how we are all interconnected, and in doing so, we nurture empathy toward others while supporting our own well-being. The teachings may be timeless, but through innovative technology they are receiving new packaging.

References

Ando, S., Clement, S., Barley, E. A., & Thornicroft, G. (2011). The simulation of hallucinations to reduce the stigma of schizophrenia: A systematic review. *Schizophrenia Research, 133*(1–3), 8–16.

Brown, S. (2020). The effectiveness of two potential mass media interventions on stigma: Video-recorded social contact and audio/visual simulations. *Community Mental Health Journal, 56*(3), 471–477.

CNN. (2014). Anderson Cooper tries a schizophrenia simulator. https://www.youtube.com/watch?v=yL9UJVtgPZY

Ferchaud, A., Seibert, J., Sellers, N., & Escobar Salazar, N. (2020). Reducing mental health stigma through identification with video game avatars with mental illness. *Frontiers in Psychology, 11*, 2240.

Galinsky, A. D., Ku, G., & Wang, C. S. (2005). Perspective-taking and self-other overlap: Fostering social bonds and facilitating social coordination. *Group Processes & Intergroup Relations, 8*(2), 109–124.

Games for Change. (2022a). Darfur is dying. https://www.gamesforchange.org/game/darfur-is-dying/

Games for Change. (2022b). Sweatshop. https://www.gamesforchange.org/game/sweatshop/

Green, M. C., & Brock, T. C. (2000). The role of transportation in the persuasiveness of public narratives. *Journal of Personality and Social Psychology, 79*(5), 701.

Herrera, F., Bailenson, J., Weisz, E., Ogle, E., & Zaki, J. (2018). Building long-term empathy: A large-scale comparison of traditional and virtual reality perspective-taking. *PloS One, 13*(10), e0204494.

Kalyanaraman, S., Penn, D. L., Ivory, J. D., & Judge, A. (2010). The virtual doppelganger: Effects of a virtual reality simulator on perceptions of schizophrenia. *The Journal of Nervous and Mental Disease, 198*(6), 437–443.

Ma, Z., & Nan, X. (2018). Role of narratives in promoting mental illnesses acceptance. *Atlantic Journal of Communication, 26*(3), 196–209.

Mann, C. E., & Himelein, M. J. (2008). Putting the person back into psychopathology: An intervention to reduce mental illness stigma in the classroom. *Social Psychiatry and Psychiatric Epidemiology, 43*(7), 545–551.

Martinez, L. R., Xu, S., & Hebl, M. (2018). Utilizing education and perspective taking to remediate the stigma of taking antidepressants. *Community Mental Health Journal, 54*(4), 450–459.

Mullor, D., Sayans-Jiménez, P., Cangas, A. J., & Navarro, N. (2019). Effect of a Serious Game (Stigma-Stop) on reducing stigma among Psychology students: A controlled study. *Cyberpsychology, Behavior, and Social Networking, 22*(3), 205–211.

Na, J. J., & Chasteen, A. L. (2016). Does imagery reduce stigma against depression? Testing the efficacy of imagined contact and perspective-taking. *Journal of Applied Social Psychology, 46*(5), 259–275.

Parrott, S., Carpentier, F. R. D., & Northup, C. T. (2017). A test of interactive narrative as a tool against prejudice. *Howard Journal of Communications, 28*(4), 374–389.

Schlote, E., & Major, A. (2021). Playing with mental issues-entertaining video games as a means for mental health education?. *Digital Culture & Education, 13*(2), 94–110.

Skorinko, J. L., & Sinclair, S. A. (2013). Perspective taking can increase stereotyping: The role of apparent stereotype confirmation. *Journal of Experimental Social Psychology, 49*(1), 10–18.

Stelzmann, D., Toth, R., & Schieferdecker, D. (2021). Can intergroup contact in virtual reality (VR) reduce stigmatization against people with schizophrenia? *Journal of Clinical Medicine, 10*(13), 2961.

Urban Ministries of Durham. (2022). Play spent. https://www.umdurham.org/spent.html

Ventura, S., Badenes-Ribera, L., Herrero, R., Cebolla, A., Galiana, L., & Baños, R. (2020). Virtual reality as a medium to elicit empathy: A meta-analysis. *Cyberpsychology, Behavior, and Social Networking, 23*(10), 667–676.

Yuen, A. S., & Mak, W. W. (2021). The effects of immersive virtual reality in reducing public stigma of mental illness in the university population of Hong Kong: Randomized controlled trial. *Journal of Medical Internet Research, 23*(7), e23683.

12

The Song (No Longer) Remains the Same: Mental Health Messages in Music

Logic, an American rapper, heard it again and again when he toured the United States, meeting fans from Los Angeles to New York. "Your music saved my life," fans would say. He would thank the fan, give them a hug, and, sometimes, admire his lyrics tattooed on their arms.

"I was like, 'Man I wasn't even trying to save nobody's life,'" Logic recalled to the website *Genius* (2017). "And then it hit me, the power that I have as an artist with a voice. I wasn't even trying to save your life. Now what can happen if I actually did?"

The epiphany led to the months-long creation of the song "1-800-273-8255," named after the telephone number for the National Suicide Prevention Lifeline in the United States. The song, performed with Alessia Cara and Khalid, follows the ruminations of a person who feels alone and longs for death, repeating "I don't wanna be alive, I just wanna die, and let me tell you why." As the song progresses, the narrator phones the crisis line and speaks with Cara, who responds, "I want you to be alive, you don't gotta die, now lemme tell you why." In the end, the narrator sees a glimmer of hope, singing "I finally wanna be alive."

"1-800-273-8255" earned a Grammy Award nomination for Best Song and reached No. 3 on the Billboard Hot 100 charts. Its accompanying music video, cast with renowned actors such as Don Cheadle, generated more than 432 million views on YouTube and another Grammy nomination. Most important, "1-800-273-8255" generated conversation about mental health and suicide prevention. In the days following the song's release, calls to the suicide prevention hotline increased more than 27% while visits to its website rose by 100,000. The Lifeline later thanked Logic on social media, saying "thank you . . . for opening up about your own struggles and for spreading hope and awareness through your music" (2017).

Parents, politicians, and other critics have long feared the potentially negative influence of popular songs and musicians on adolescents, bemoaning hidden messages, implicit meanings, and explicit content. Protestors burned records by The Beatles. Police threatened to arrest record store owners who sold 2 Live Crew's *As Nasty As They Wanna Be.* When it comes to mental health, lawyers have sued musicians for the deaths of teenagers and blamed Goth rock for mass shootings. Increasingly, though, we are recognizing the potentially positive outcomes of music—both playing and listening—on mental health and stigma.

Researchers in musicology, psychology, and other fields have studied the effect of music on listener's thoughts and emotions. Music contains rhythm and repetition, which engages the neocortex of the brain, calming the listener. We can use music to manage our moods, blasting rock music to get ready for a football game or listening to sad love songs after a break-up. In psychology, experiments have shown the potential for music to increase concentration and cognitive processing (e.g., Angel et al., 2010) and to decrease stress and anxiety (e.g., Chan et al., 2003).

This chapter focuses on the stigma-related outcomes of music. Specifically, the chapter uses anecdotal and empirical evidence to illustrate how musicians can use songs and personal disclosures to challenge stigma and support mental health among music fans. Musicians and the songs they create have the power to reduce social isolation, inspire healthy behaviour, nurture empathy, and play an influential role in mitigating stigma.

Mental Health in Music Lyrics

Musicians have long discussed mental health in song lyrics, sharing struggles caused by spurned love, social exclusion, family conflict, and other stressors. The songs cross genres from pop to punk, and rap to rock. Backed by instrumentals melancholy or upbeat, loud or soothing, musicians have used lyrics to shares stories of anxiety, depression, and even suicidal contemplations. Some songs are explicit, seemingly conveying calls for help—take, for example, Notorious B.I.G.'s "Suicidal Thoughts" or Nirvana's "I Hate Myself and I Want to Die"—while others are ambiguous about suicidal intent while illustrating the isolation, fear, and even anger one can experience because of illness—see/hear Pearl Jam's "Jeremy." Together, the songs represent a catalogue of artistic expression that permits all listeners to recognize the importance of mental health. Songs have the power to reach people everywhere from the car to the grocery store, and their musical and lyrical content can inspire listeners, improve moods, and perhaps challenge the stigma of mental illness by illustrating how depression, anxiety, and other conditions can affect anyone, even people at the pinnacle of stardom.

Whether country songs or hip-hop tracks, blues standards or Gospel records, popular music often communicates stories of people either overcoming or succumbing to worldly pressures. The songs are too numerous to list. To illustrate the range of material, though, first consider the work of Leroy Carr, a prolific Depression-era blues musician, who minced no words when he recorded "Suicide Blues" in the winter of 1934 and spring of 1935. "If somebody finds me, when I'm dead and gone/Say I did self-murder, I died with my boots on," Carr sang. "No I ain't no coward, and I'll tell you why/I just was tired of living, but wasn't afraid to die."

"Ready to Die" was the title of the debut studio album of The Notorious B.I.G., a modern classic released 59 years after Leroy Carr's early death from alcoholism. On the album's 17th track, Christopher Wallace, also known as Biggie Smalls, shared his "Suicidal Thoughts" with a friend over the phone, rapping "I swear to God I just want to slit my wrists and end this bullshit/Throw the Magnum to my head, threaten to pull shit/And squeeze until the bed's completely red." As the song progresses, his friend transitions from being annoyed by the late night call to frantically rushing for help. He is too late, though, as the song ends with the friend screaming Biggie's name into the phone, a gunshot, and the fading thump of a dying heart.

Music can convey and elicit emotion from a diverse audience, connecting with listeners regardless of race, age, gender, or income. Well-crafted songs capture shared human experience while remaining open to interpretation concerning the artist's intended message. For example, Leroy Carr's record label never released the song "Suicide Blues," apparently believing its description of a man happy to be dead would not resonate with audiences. One need only look at the number of songs labelled "Suicide Blues" to appreciate that people can relate to songs bemoaning the trials of life and begging for release. Lightnin' Hopkins asked for directions to the Red River because he wanted to "go floating down the stream, cause there ain't no room, poor Lightnin's done." Stringbean, a banjo-picking star of the Grand Ole Opry, declared he would "whittle myself a little wooden gun, and blow my brains out just for fun, and kill myself, oh Lordy, me."

What happens when people hear such songs? As with other media effects, the results can be complicated. Musicians who discuss depression, anxiety, suicidal thoughts, and other challenges can inspire hope or risk based on listeners' interpretations. Metal musician Ozzy Osbourne released "Suicide Solution," which he called an anti-suicide composition about another musician who drank himself to death (Reuters, 1986). Despite his professed intentions, Osbourne ended up in court over the song when a 19-year-old California teen shot himself to death while listening to the album. His parents claimed the record contained a hidden message of "Get the gun and try it, shoot, shoot, shoot." Osbourne said the song contained no hidden message. A similar case emerged when Blink 182 walked listeners through the contemplations of a suicidal teenager in "Adam's Song," singing "I never thought I'd die alone/Another six months I'll be unknown/Give all my things to all my friends/You'll never step foot in my room again" (NPR, 2018). The song reached the top 25 on charts in three countries, including No. 2 on U.S. Billboard Hot Modern Rock Tracks. Similar to Osbourne's "Suicide Solution," Blink 182 described the song as well-intentioned, a song designed to inspire hope. It did, for some. An elementary school teacher wanted the first three notes tattooed on his body because the song helped him through difficult times, he told National Public Radio (NPR, 2018). Another fan said the song helped her emotionally process a friend's suicide. "Adam's Song" resembled "Suicide Solution" in another way, however, when a teenager died by suicide while listening to the track on repeat. The songs illustrate the potential for musicians to encounter outrage and controversy when using music to navigate subjects such as suicide, depression, and mental illness. They also illustrate potentially negative outcomes.

Still, there are a growing number of cases in which musicians are using their positions and art to nurture healthy conversations about mental health, openly challenging stigma and encouraging fans to talk about depression, anxiety, and other illnesses. When it comes to art, musicians are crafting hit songs in which they convey what it feels like to have a mental illness. The songs are garnering not only popularity, critical acclaim, and financial success, but appreciation from fans who went through similar experiences. To illustrate, international star Ariana Grande captured the experience of anxiety on "Breathin' " when she sang "Feel my blood runnin', swear the sky's fallin'/How do I know if this shit's fabricated, oh?" Fans appreciated the song and its accompanying music video, which has more than 220 million views on YouTube. One person wrote, "This song really helped (with anxiety), I'd listen on repeat while forcing myself to do things my brain was telling me was unsafe. Fighting a panic attack in a grocery store but I'd keep breathin." Another wrote, "I started suffering mental illness . . . now I can feel this song more than everything. . . . we are stronger than anxiety, we are STRONG."

At times, lyrics contain subtle messages concerning mental illness but still resonate. For example, the Seattle band Pearl Jam gained international attention with the release of "Jeremy," a song in which a bullied and isolated boy dies by suicide. Suicide is never explicitly referenced. In the song's chorus, singer Eddie Vedder howls, "Jeremy spoke in class today." A music video for the song generated controversy because it showed Jeremy tossing an apple to a teacher before shooting himself in the head. Censoring Jeremy's death did little to help, increasing the ambiguity of the video and making it appear the teen shot his classmates. They cowered in frozen shock, covered in blood. Political pundits, parents, and other commenters were quick to condemn the video, criticizing the content as harmful for vulnerable teens. However, music fans also related to Jeremy, his sense of isolation, and his experiences with bullying. The official video, which has 133 million views on YouTube, currently requires viewers to click a consent statement acknowledging that "The following content may contain suicide or self-harm topics."

During the same period, Nirvana became one of the most influential rock bands of all time. The band's lead singer, Kurt Cobain, often referenced mental illness in lyrics and song titles, including the international hit Lithium, named after anti-depressant medication. The lyrics for Lithium mimicked manic depression by alternating between highs and lows: "I'm so happy, because today, I found my friends. They're in my head." Another interpretation describes the song as a narrator trying to appear happy when in fact he is depressed. In 1993, Cobain was more explicit when the band recorded "I Hate Myself and Want to Die," with the chorus, "End it someday/What's that sound?" The band initially discarded "I Hate Myself . . . " as the title for their album *in utero* because they figured people would not understand the attempt at dark humor (Rolling Stone, 2021). Cobain died by suicide seven months after the song's release. It was one of several songs during the so-called grunge era to directly reference suicide. Silverchair, an Australian band, released "Suicidal Dream" in which Daniel Johns sings "Help me, comfort me/Stop me from feeling what I'm feeling now/The rope is here, now I'll find a use/I kill myself, I put my head in a noose."

Contrasting the 1990s, the modern era of popular music is one in which musicians challenge stereotypes by sharing their personal experiences and conveying hope. Demi Lovato, who has publicly disclosed her experience with bipolar disorder, adopts a defiant tone in the song "Skyscraper," telling an antagonist that she "will be rising from the ground/like a skyscraper." Singer Rachel Platten declares, "This is my fight song, my take back my life song," in her No. 1 pop song from 2014. Two years later, Scott "Kid Cudi" Mercudi released "Wounds," in which the hip hop artist told listeners, "We all have times when we weep/It's a troubled life, traumatized psychologically," before reaching a chorus in which he declares, "I'ma sew these wounds, I-I'ma sew these wounds myself."

Researchers are studying the representation of mental health and illness in popular music and noting the change. Alex Kresovich and colleagues (2021) examined the lyrics of 125 rap songs from five years—1998, 2003, 2008, 2013, and 2018. The research team wanted to know how often rappers referenced anxiety, depression, suicide, and other subjects related to mental health. References to mental health increased during the time period, as rappers discussed struggles with love, life, and other stressors.

"This increase is important, given that rap artists serve as role models to their audience, which (includes) US young people across strata, constituting a large group with increased risk of mental health issues and under-use of mental health services," Kresovich and colleagues write (p. 289).

Indeed, beyond emotional reactions, young fans can model the attitudes, behaviors, and aspirations of famous musicians. From rappers to rock stars, musicians shape popular culture by influencing the way people dress, talk, and behave in other ways. The social cognitive theory of mass communication (Bandura, 2009) suggests youth would be inclined to copy behavior they consider rewarding after witnessing the example of musicians they emulate. Fans also develop parasocial relationships with musicians (Kurtin et al., 2019). Given the literature, we can anticipate that a popular musician who shares testimony concerning mental health can be especially influential. A musician's behaviour, such as seeking and benefiting from treatment, might also be persuasive.

Testimonials by Popular Musicians

In addition to lyrics, musicians are sharing personal experience with mental illness through interviews, public service announcements, and other avenues. Musicians call out stereotypes, challenge notions concerning whom mental illness affects, educate fans about mental health resources, and encourage followers to seek treatment, discuss mental health, and know they are not alone. Social media affords musicians the opportunity to bypass traditional news outlets and directly address fans and followers.

Ariana Grande experienced post traumatic stress after terrorists attacked her concert at the Manchester Arena in 2017, murdering 22 people (Sorto, 2019). The singer openly discusses the role of therapy in her recovery and continued well-being, recommending it to millions of followers on social media. "Therapy has saved my life so many times," she tweeted. "If you're afraid to ask for help, don't be. You don't have to be in constant pain and you can process trauma. I've got a lot of work to do but it's a start to even be aware that it's possible." In June 2021, Grande donated $1 million of free therapy to her fans (Sheidlower, 2021).

Scott "Kid Cudi" Mescudi, who shared messages about mental health in his songs, once used social media to inform fans he was checking into rehab for "depression and suicidal urges." "I am not at peace," he wrote. "I haven't been since you've known me. If I didn't come here, I would've done something to myself." In the letter, Mescudi described being unable to leave his house and make new friends because "my anxiety and depression have ruled my life for as long as I can remember." In addition to his initial disclosure, Mescudi later shared news concerning his recovery. In a cover story with *Billboard*, Mescudi said "I'm the best I've ever been in my life." Describing the initial disclosure, he said he "saw that the response was all love and support, and it really touched me" (Holmes, 2018, para. 5).

James Blake, an English musician, used social media to persuade his fans to be open about mental health (Snapes, 2018). The call for action followed the release of his song "Don't Miss It," which people described as "sad boy." Blake condemned the "unhealthy and problematic" description (para. 7), saying that the characterization "contributes to the ever disastrous historical stigmatisation of men expressing themselves emotionally." Silence has repercussions for mental health, the singer told fans, and "There is no great victory in machismo and bravado … The road to mental health and happiness, which I feel so passionately about, is paved with honesty."

Outcomes of Songs and Disclosures

There is anecdotal evidence that songs can improve people's attitudes toward mental health, including the fans who described connecting with Blink 182's "Adam's

Song" to NPR. Songs and testimonials show potential in four key areas: reducing isolation among listeners; spurring information-seeking and -sharing; providing positive mental health role models; and educating the public about symptoms, conditions, and treatments. In addition, there is evidence that artistic expression, including the creation of music, can challenge self-stigma by empowering an artist (e.g., Gaiha et al., 2021).

First, musicians can show people who are affected by mental illness that they are not alone, reducing listeners' sense of isolation. A pseudo connection often develops between celebrities and fans, a false sense in which the fan feels they "know" the artist despite lacking any direct connection. A listener might strongly relate to a singer's lyrics and see a bit of themselves in the artist. A person who previously felt isolated—because of bad social experiences at school, a sense of disconnection from family, or another factor—may suddenly feel as though someone they respect went through similar travails and survived. To illustrate, Silverchair, the Australian rock band, released a song called "Ana's Song (Open Fire)," which described lead singer Daniel Johns' experiences with eating disorders. At times growling, at times whimpering, Johns sings, "Ana wrecks your life/like an anorexia life." At present, the music video for the song has more than 9 million views on YouTube (Silverchair, 2011), where it generated comments such as: "I struggle from anorexia nervosa myself and am now focusing on recovering. I relate to Johns' lyrics so much. Very emotional song and so strong and powerful." In another example, as related in Chapter 6, professional basketball player DeMar DeRozan quoted a rap song by Kevin Gates when he disclosed his experience with depression on social media, writing "This depression get the best of me."

Second, disclosures by musicians and the resultant news coverage can inspire information-seeking and -sharing by listeners whose interest in mental health becomes piqued. Popular songs generate headlines, listens, downloads, and millions of views through music videos online. A person who hears Kid Cudi rap about depression might question whether their own bad moods, exhaustion, and disinterest could be an indicator of the illness. The music fan might seek out information through Internet sources, professional experts, social media, and other outlets. Backing the idea, Francis (2018) surveyed 182 Black men one month after Mescudi's disclosure to see whether the extent to which they identified with the musician, their emotions after hearing about the disclosure, and their own experiences with depression symptoms predicted information-seeking behaviour. Francis found a relationship. The more men identified with Kid Cudi, the more they reacted emotionally to his disclosure. The stronger the emotional distress, the greater the time men spent seeking information about depression. In addition to information-seeking, in comment sections of music videos fans express appreciation for artists' disclosures and, inspired, share their own stories of mental health. A community of commenters can develop from the initial disclosure, as one person's story inspires another to ask questions, which encourages other commenters to respond, nurturing an online dialogue about mental health beneath a music video with 9 million views.

Third, fans who emulate musicians may vicariously learn through their example; a listener might be encouraged to seek therapy when a musician says it can help. Fans consider musicians role models from whom they might learn valuable lessons about what to do—and what not to do—in life. When musicians share pro-active messages about mental health, the songs might nurture positive attitudes and behaviour. In mass communication theory, social learning is a phenomenon in which we learn through the example of others. If someone encounters positive results by behaving a certain way, we are inclined to copy the behavior because it pays off. If someone encounters negative outcomes, or no real rewards, we might avoid performing the behavior. When a musician such as Kid Cudi shares the positive outcomes of therapy, describing himself as happier than ever, fans might consider therapy themselves because they see it paid off for someone they respect.

Fourth, musicians can correct misguided assumptions concerning mental illness, educating fans, challenging stereotypes, and bucking Western notions of professional and personal success. Kresovich (2018) sought to understand how popular music might improve listeners' (a) attitudes toward people with mental illness, (b) mental health stigma, (c) support for public mental health resources, (d) willingness to help people who experience struggles, and (e) inclination toward seeking mental health treatment. People who personally connected with the song or musician subsequently reported more positive attitudes, except when it came to seeking help themselves. Still, respondents did report an increased likelihood of "dealing with their own mental health issues" when they connected to the song.

In addition to challenging public stigma, the creation of music appears to be beneficial for people's attitudes toward themselves. Shivani Mathur Gaiha and colleagues (2021) reviewed 57 studies in which researchers used the arts to target the stigmatization of mental illness. In some studies, people created art, making movies, writing songs. In other studies, people encountered art, watching movies, listening to songs. The evidence remained inconclusive because studies lacked strong design, but overall it appeared that the arts interventions helped improve attitudes concerning mental health. Providing further evidence, a hospital in Colorado launched a board in which area youth partnered with adult mentors to create mental health advocacy campaigns (Kennedy et al., 2020). The youths used the arts, including songwriting, to communicate personal stories about mental illness. They described the artistic expression as empowering, saying they learned about mental health, felt good about themselves, and effectively engaged other high school and college students in storytelling about mental health.

Conclusion

Music is all around us: People listen to songs while jogging, walking to class, driving to work, shopping in the grocery store. Messages about mental health have long appeared in music, from old blues standards to modern pop, and only recently have mental health advocates and researchers sought to understand how music might challenge public and self-stigma related to mental illness. There is much research to be done. However, the initial results are promising. Indeed, in 2021, an international team of researchers published a study the British Medical Journal in which they examined the influence of Logic's 1–800 song (Niederkrotenthaler et al., 2021). The rapper performed the song during the 60th Annual Grammy Awards and the MTV Music Awards. During the MTV performance, Logic stood surrounded by people affected by suicide. They wore shirts that included the number and a message: "You are not alone." As witnessed after the song's release, phone calls, the researchers found, increased to the hotline in the days that followed the live performances, underscoring the potential for music to challenge the silence surrounding mental illness—and possibly save a life.

References

Angel, L. A., Polzella, D. J., & Elvers, G. C. (2010). Background music and cognitive performance. *Perceptual and Motor Skills, 110*(3_suppl), 1059–1064.

Bandura, A. (2009). Social cognitive theory of mass communication. In J. Bryant, & M. B. Oliver, *Media effects: Advances in theory and research* (pp. 110–140). Routledge.

Chan, Y. M., Lee, P. W., Ng, T. Y., Ngan, H. Y., & Wong, L. C. (2003). The use of music to reduce anxiety for patients undergoing colposcopy: A randomized trial. *Gynecologic Oncology, 91*(1), 213–217.

Francis, D. B. (2018). Young Black men's information seeking following celebrity depression disclosure: Implications for mental health communication. *Journal of Health Communication, 23*(7), 687–694.

Gaiha, S. M., Salisbury, T. T., Usmani, S., Koschorke, M., Raman, U., & Petticrew, M. (2021). Effectiveness of arts interventions to reduce mental-health-related stigma among youth: A systematic review and meta-analysis. *BMC Psychiatry, 21*(1), 1–26.

Genius (2017). Logic "1-800-273-8255" official lyrics and meaning, verified. https://www.youtube.com/watch?v=SOJTg9cL5bM&t=18s

Holmes, C. (2018, July 19). Kid Cudi says he's 'reborn' after going to rehab for 'suicidal urges.' MTV News. https://www.mtv.com/news/3082477/kid-cudi-reborn-suicidal-urges/

Kennedy, H., Marley, M., Torres, K., Edelblute, A., & Novins, D. (2020). "Be creative and you will reach more people": Youth's experiences participating in an arts-based social action group aimed at mental health stigma reduction. *Arts & Health, 12*(1), 23–37.

Kreps, D. (2016). Kid Cudi checks into rehab for depression, 'suicidal urges' Rolling Stone. https://www.rollingstone.com/music/music-news/kid-cudi-checks-into-rehab-for-depression-suicidal-urges-112754/

Kresovich, A. (2020). The influence of pop songs referencing anxiety, depression, and suicidal ideation on college students' mental health empathy, stigma, and behavioral intentions. *Health Communication, 37*(5), 617–627.

Kresovich, A., Collins, M. K. R., Riffe, D., & Carpentier, F. R. D. (2021). A content analysis of mental health discourse in popular rap music. *JAMA Pediatrics, 175*(3), 286–292.Kurtin, K. S., O'Brien, N. F., Roy, D., & Dam, L. (2019). Parasocial relationships with musicians. *The Journal of Social Media in Society, 8*(2), 30–50.

National Suicide Prevention Lifeline. (2017). https://twitter.com/800273TALK/status/857618456879009792

Niederkrotenthaler, T., Tran, U. S., Gould, M., Sinyor, M., Sumner, S., Strauss, M. J., . . . & Draper, J. (2021). Association of Logic's hip hop song "1-800-273-8255" with Lifeline calls and suicides in the United States: interrupted time series analysis. *BMJ, 375*, 1–8.

NPR. (2018). The legacy of 'Adam's Song,' an anthem to darkness, loss – and recovery. NPR. https://www.npr.org/2018/10/04/653632962/blink-182-adam-song-american-anthem-darkness-loss-recovery

Reuters. (1986). Around the nation; Court throws out suit against Ozzy Osbourne. The New York Times. https://www.nytimes.com/1986/08/08/us/around-the-nation-court-throws-out-suit-against-ozzy-osbourne.html

Rolling Stone. (2021). No apologies: All 102 Nirvana songs ranked. https://au.rollingstone.com/music/music-lists/no-apologies-all-102-nirvana-songs-ranked-26796/i-hate-myself-and-want-to-die-26856/

Sheidlower, N. (2021). Ariana Grande giving away $1M worth of therapy to fans. *New York Post.* https://nypost.com/2021/06/30/ariana-grande-giving-away-1m-worth-of-therapy-to-fans/

Silverchair. (2011). Ana's song (Open fire) (Official video). https://www.youtube.com/watch?v=zNK_r2QAXAo

Snapes, L. (2018). James Blake speaks out about struggle with depression. *The Guardian*. https://www.theguardian.com/music/2018/jul/03/james-blake-speaks-out-about-struggle-with-depression

Sorto, G. (2019). Ariana Grande shares brain scan and opens up about PTSD. *CNN*. https://www.cnn.com/2019/04/12/entertainment/ariana-grande-ptsd-brain-scan-instagram-trnd/index.html

13

What Can We Do? Conclusions and Action Items

Curiosity got the best of me one recent afternoon. My colleagues shared a digital tool with me, one advertisers use to "listen" to online conversations about their products. It is the type of software that Ford could use to learn what people are saying on Twitter about its new electric truck, or McDonald's could use to understand how customers are chatting on Facebook about the McRib. Instead of searching for a sandwich or pickup, I punched the word "stigma" into the system, clicked enter, and watched the digital wheels spin.

Within seconds, I could see everything from the number of times "stigma" was mentioned on Facebook and Twitter in 2021 (3.36 million) to the number of people those posts reached through friends and followers (31.4 billion). I could see where the digital conversations were happening (mostly in the United States, Canada, and United Kingdom) and the gender of the social media users (55% female, 45% male). Perhaps most interesting, the system displayed the content of the posts. Hundreds of thousands of people were using social media to challenge the stigma attached to mental illness, debunking stereotypes about medication, educating people about autism, calling for mental health resources from elected leaders, and using the platforms to advocate for social change. For example, one man on Twitter described how a new medication and mindset had been life-changing, writing, "Don't be afraid to ask for help if you need it, especially men. We NEED to break the stigma . . . "

Though anecdotal, the social media posts illustrate the sea change we are witnessing in relation to mental health and stigma. People are using mass media, especially social platforms, to challenge inaccurate information, educate the public, and protest stigma. As this book illustrates, we are also witnessing a paradigm shift in terms of research, as scholars transition from studying how media content *perpetuates* stigma to how it might *challenge* stereotypes, prejudice, and discrimination. The problem exists; how can it be fixed? How might we flip the script and use news stories, movies, novels, songs, video games, and other mass media to educate, elicit empathy, and demonstrate support? How might mass media help, rather than harm? The evidence covered in this book suggests four umbrella action items, at least, as well as gaps in the research literature that scholars can work to plug. This final chapter presents those suggestions and directions for future study.

Action Item No. 1: Pull Back the Curtain

We can mistakenly romanticize newsrooms and Hollywood. In reality, the people who create our news content, television, movies, and music follow predictable schedules and routines much the same as any 9-to-5 worker. By pulling back the curtain as Toto did in the *Wizard of Oz*, we can understand the motivations of journalists, scriptwriters, producers, and even social media influencers, subsequently identifying (a) problems and (b) solutions in relation to the portrayal of mental health. The key is understanding how personal attitudes, organizational structure, social norms, profit motives, and other identifiable factors influence the creation and dissemination of media content.

Take the work of the National Alliance on Mental Illness. The organization, based in the United States, advocates for mental health by proposing governmental policy, calling for improved care, sharing educational information about symptoms and treatment, and even inserting itself into journalistic routines. NAMI provides journalists resources and recommendations on how they can craft responsible news stories. The NAMI website (https://www.nami.org/Press-Media) provides research updates concerning mental health, statistics, information graphics, and a directory of sources that journalists can easily tap when reporting about mental health. It lists contact information for sources, who are important voices in the stories journalists tell. NAMI also proactively shares formal statements during major news events such as the 2022 mass murder of schoolchildren in Uvalde, Texas. In that case, the organization challenged Republican framing of the crime that pointed toward mental illness as the primary factor for the violence. NAMI blamed firearm access and wrote that "People across the globe live with mental illness, but only in the U.S. do we have an epidemic of senseless and tragic mass shootings" (NAMI, 2022, para. 3). Mental health advocates who understand how journalists work stand better chance of seeing proactive messages in print. Indeed, journalists across the country picked up NAMI's statement concerning the mass shooting and printed the comment word-for-word (e.g., Mitropoulos, 2022). Thus, an understanding of production routines also helps advocates minimize the harm of negative messages by being proactive.

When stereotypes or misinformation do emerge, mental health advocates can respond by reaching out to the reporter, writer, or producer responsible for the content and educating them about the problem. Education might prevent future errors. When content creators are unresponsive, advocates might find success by reaching out to the people who control the pocketbooks—advertisers and administrators. NAMI has adopted such a dual approach, directly reaching out to Hollywood producers before publicly calling for changes to television shows or movies.

Partnership appears to work. A number of initiatives, including Reporting on Suicide and the Entertainment Industries Council, are working alongside writers, directors, and other creators to improve content. Five values direct the work of the Entertainment Industries Council, including the adoption of a "non-judgmental approach" and recognition that "members of the entertainment industry make a variety of positive contributions addressing health and social issues" (EIC, 2022, para. 5). In one initiative, EIC offers writers, producers, and actors a "First Draft" review, connecting the creators with experts in mental health.

The "First Draft" program illustrates one way in which advocates can challenge stereotypes by becoming involved in the front end of content creation. Advocates can also develop relationships with journalists, pitching story ideas and stepping up as sources when a reporter is covering mental health or related subjects. The reporters, photographers, and editors who work for local newspapers and television outlets throughout the United States are called community journalists; without community, their jobs would be impossible. Therefore, these journalists are generally open to meeting new sources whose expertise can be tapped when newsworthy issues arise. Advocates should actively develop working relationships with local journalists, connecting journalists with sources, story ideas, and other information that would help provide context and alternative angles to stories about mental health.

Such relationships are important if advocates want news outlets to consider mental health an important subject, which often translates into an issue also appearing important to the public. A growing number of advocacy organizations are understanding the importance of mass media campaigns in identifying issues facing mental health care, generating public interest in topics and applying pressure to politicians and other decision-makers. For example, the rise of social media has afforded advocates the power to influence the media, public, and policy agendas by reaching millions of people quickly with minimal cost. Hashtags such as #BlackMindsMatter illustrate how grassroots initiatives can generate dialogue about mental health while highlighting community issues. In addition to kickstarting dialogue, advocates would do well to remain positive while engaging audiences via social media, an environment that might resemble the muck-and-mire of a swamp given the toxicity that shrouds health and political issues at times. Advocates should focus on empowerment, sharing information that will help people navigate times of crisis, enhance self-esteem, and communicate uplifting stories about life with mental illness. By no means does this recommendation mean ignoring problems, including those related to insurance, treatment access/quality, and stigma. Instead, advocates should borrow a page from reporters who practice "solutions journalism." Rather than simply describing problems, solutions journalists also recommend approaches by which the problems might be addressed or even solved.

By understanding the mechanisms behind the news, mental health advocates can anticipate how journalists will respond to events on the local, state, and national levels. When news breaks on the national level, advocates can reach out to community journalists with recommendations for sources or messages that provide context. In doing so, they can forestall stereotypical or problematic stories. NAMI demonstrated such tactics in the aftermath of the 2022 Uvalde elementary school shooting; advocates openly condemned access to firearms while explaining to television viewers that people with mental illness are rarely violent toward others.

Journalists might also help community reporters "localize" national events by sharing source and story ideas that would help challenge the stigma of mental illness. For example, journalists were drawn to cover the COVID-19 pandemic in 2020–2022 given its ramifications for health, education, economy, equality, and other areas of daily life. Mental health advocates engaged local journalists to provide readers stories focused on solutions. How might parents buoy children's mental health during this trying period? What protective factors can we adopt during such anxious times? To illustrate, the United Nations International Children's Emergency Fund, or UNICEF, published a news release headlined, "How teenagers can protect their mental health during COVID-19," in which health professionals shared six tips for teenagers such as "anxiety is normal" and "feel your feelings," (UNICEF, 2020). Such stories are not only helpful, they engage the public in proactive conversation about mental health, representing an indirect method for challenging stigma.

When it comes to research, the field needs insight into the processes behind the creation of media content about mental health. Recent studies detailed the challenges and opportunities faced by journalists who cover mental health. But we lack modern studies that draw back the curtain on the creation of movies, television shows, and other fare. It would be helpful to have scholarship that illustrates how individual, social, financial, and other factors shape the creation of media content about mental health. At the same time, society would benefit from studies that examine which mental health items appear on the public, media, and policy agendas—and why. Scholars have described how corporations manipulate these agendas for financial gain. Such knowledge can help people avoid being exploited, while also identifying best practices for ensuring prosocial messages related to mental health elicit the attention they deserve.

Action Item No. 2: Support Disclosures

In 2018, Harper's Bazaar published a story headlined, "39 celebrities who have opened up about mental health" (Roberts, 2018). Declaring the disclosures "proof that anxiety and depression can affect anyone," the story provided images and summaries of actors, actresses, singers, and writers who dealt with anxiety and depression. There was Beyonce, an international superstar singer whose mother told her to care for her mental health; Dakota Johnson, an American actress who experienced panic attacks; and Jared Padalecki, an actor who described himself as "passionate about people dealing with mental illness and struggling with depression, or addiction, or having suicidal thoughts," because he had navigated comparable experiences (2018, para. 15).

Such disclosures are important because they help normalize conversations about mental health. Equally important are public responses to the disclosures. In one study, my colleagues and I examined how fans responded to the mental health disclosures of DeMar DeRozan and Kevin Love, two professional basketball players in the United States (Parrott et al., 2020). The responses were generally positive, as thousands of fans praised the players for sharing, disclosed their own experiences with mental illness, and called for an end to stigma. Such responses are important because they illustrate for society—and other celebrities—that disclosures should be applauded rather than condemned.

Disclosures are individual decisions; a person should weigh the pros and cons of coming out because they could indeed encounter prejudice and discrimination in personal relationships, school settings, or employment. People who choose to broadcast their experience with depression, anxiety, or another illness are taking a significant step—and should be respected for the decision. This goes for celebrities.

As advertisers appreciate, celebrity cameos are one of the best ways to generate public interest in places, products, and even public health. A growing number of athletes, actors, musicians, and other celebrities are sharing personal experience with mental health issues such as depression, anxiety, and bipolar disorder. The testimonials, often delivered via social media, can challenge stigma in several ways. Celebrity disclosures reinforce the fact mental illness can affect anyone, regardless of race, gender, age, income, or professional success. Celebrities are also good at persuasion, given their standing in society. Fans are inclined to listen to an athlete or actress when they challenge traditional beliefs, attitudes, and behaviors related to mental illness.

Still, people need not be celebrities to solicit change. People can share their own experiences with mental health while choosing the size of the audience they wish to engage. It could be anyone on social media, or an individual's close friends and family. In addition, mental health advocates can help challenge stigma by connecting journalists and other storytellers with people who are actually affected by disorders. By telling personal stories via the media, advocates can initiate contact with an audience member who might not otherwise "meet" a person affected by mental illness. Such contact can challenge stereotypes and prejudice, especially when it provides information that challenges false beliefs and illustrates humanity rather than symptoms.

Still, much of the enthusiasm about parasocial contact is drawn from research related to other marginalized groups such as the LGBTQ community. The field would benefit from additional scholarship, especially research that pinpoints the conditions in which contact works (or doesn't). The focus of contact appears to be important. Contact appears to work best when it conveys the humanity—rather than the symptoms—of a person who has experienced mental illness. Still, we need empirical data to support or refute the explanation.

Action Item No. 3: Connect Online

"Yesterday I had a severe panic attack."

This is how a young woman began her social media post as she sought advice from an online support group for people who experience depression and anxiety. Within minutes, she received responses from the group's 70,000+ members in which people offered sympathy and sound medical advice.

"Does anyone want to talk?"

A young man made this statement. Instead of advice, he simply sought to connect with other people and turned to the group where he knew people would understand what he was going through.

Human connection is important for mental health, and a growing number of people are turning to online communities to find answers to questions and develop relationships they otherwise lack. People who are knowledgeable about mental health, whether medical professionals or advocates, can offer support to people who might be puzzled or stressed about the issues they are facing. Online communities also offer people morale support, illustrating they are not alone or "odd" for experiencing a mental health issue.

The omnipresence of social media in modern life means people have greater access to other people, for better or worse. On one hand, social connections can buoy the amount of worth a person places in themselves. They can connect a person with sound medical advice, answer questions, and alleviate concerns. On the other, the connections made online can be unhelpful or even harmful. Indeed, there is a significant challenge looming for mental health advocates and researchers. We need to identify the ways in which online communities are helpful and harmful, so best practice recommendations can be developed that will help these communities reach their full positive potential.

To illustrate, the social media platform reddit provides /r/depression, a page offering peer support for people experiencing depression. One recent afternoon, three of the top posts questioned the point of life, threatened suicide, and called hope for the future "bullshit." The posts could be helpful by permitting people to vent and seek empathy from people who have experienced similar thoughts and feelings; however, responses echoing the negative sentiment could create a downward spiral rather than ladder out of despair. Given the issue, national mental health organizations should develop volunteer networks to man popular message boards to challenge inaccurate or harmful information while sharing helpful and accurate recommendations. At the least, moderators should do better jobs intervening when posts demonstrate life-threatening sentiments.

Beyond instances of crisis, social networking sites offer the public an opportunity to challenge stigmatizing statements, policies, and beliefs in an easy and cost effective manner. Advocates can use social media to organize real-world protests related to mental health, and media savvy advocates can also drum up news coverage of the protests through relationships with journalists. Often, education is an effective approach for challenging stigma. Advocates can use media to help the public become more mental health literate, with the goal of fighting stigma by increasing knowledge.

Again, it would be helpful if researchers identified best practices. What elicits desired results, and what does not? At the moment, the scant evidence suggests that repeating stereotypes and false information about mental health might backfire, planting the information in someone's head. It appears messages will be successful when they focus on hope, illustrating how mental health issues are common and treatable.

Action Item No. 4: Embrace Digital Tools

In "The Perks of Being a Wallflower," a teenager named Charlie navigates challenges typical of high school—bullies, first love, friendship—and experiences that can be isolating and even life-threatening—depression, sexual abuse, suicidal ideations. The film won dozens of awards and nominations, including everything from "best kiss" at the MTV Movie Awards to Best Adapted Screenplay from the Writers Guild of America. A half million viewers reviewed the film on IMDb, the internet movie database, awarding it a score of 8/10 (IMDb, 2022).

The movie also received an 8/10 on the website CineWell, but the critic's review judged more than the entertainment value, authenticity, and acting of the film. Instead, Rachel B., an 18-year-old high school student, used her 2021 review to provide trigger warnings, identify mental health themes, and rate the quality with which the movie portrayed mental health (CineWell, 2021). Rachel B. wrote (para. 15):

> My friends have had struggles with suicidal ideation and while the movie doesn't glamorize it, it leaves Charlie on a very happy, fulfilled note full on hope which is not everyone's experiences with depression or having a loved one die by suicide. However, the hope at the end could be a sign to someone with depression that life gets better and to live in the moment.

The CineWell website is published by Stanford University's Media & Mental Health Initiative. It is one example of how advocacy and academic organizations are shifting their attention from identifying problems to implementing solutions for mental health stigma using novel approaches and technology. In this case, rather than protesting negative depictions, CineWell offers site visitors recommendations for entertaining—and accurate—films while providing warnings about potentially harmful content. Such films can provide viewers prosocial views of mental illness, permitting audiences to "walk a mile" in the shoes of a character affected by depression, bipolar disorder, or another condition.

Perhaps the greatest digital innovations have occurred in the world of video games. In 40 years, we have witnessed gaming technology develop from the pixelated characters of Atari to the immersive virtual reality of Oculus Rift. The gaming world also saw an increasing number of independently developed games, interactive features designed with social change in mind rather than mass profit. Instead of shoot-'em-up war games, players can adopt the perspective of characters who are navigating fantasy worlds while fighting back delusions, or adopt the perspective of a character experiencing anxiety. Such games are attracting growing support inside and outside the industry. Indeed, Microsoft recently featured "Disability and neurodiversity community games and movies" on its Xbox console (Microsoft, 2022). Gamers who clicked on the link found dozens of games and movies—many free of charge—"curated by disability and neurodiversity communities." The company described the collection as reflecting "experiences related to chronic or complex illness, hearing, mobility, speech, learning, mental health, neurodiversity, and vision." The library featured the game "Fractured Minds," described as an "immersive artistic short game" created by Emily Mitchell, 17, "with the hope of aiding understanding and awareness of mental illness." In addition to game development, the library illustrates how gamers (and others) can support digital innovation in relation to mental health. Gaming companies—such as Xbox, PlayStation, and Nintendo—can support independent game creators by hosting and advertising innovative pro-social games. They can even advertise those games, as Xbox did with its millions of users. In addition, gamers (and others) should support the studios and independent creators who design video games, interactive narratives, virtual reality experiences, and digital advocacy related to mental health and other social issues by downloading, sharing, or purchasing games. Such industry efforts should be applauded, and game designers should continue consulting mental health experts—especially people personally navigating mental illness—while designing their interactive experiences. Finally, mental health advocates can share these games through social media or other means, essentially spreading the proactive messages. Toward this end, a number of organizations such as Games for Change have begun recognizing game developers whose efforts seek to promote a better world.

Action Item No. 5: Create

The tools available now—from accessible computer animation to computer-based recording studios—mean creators have worlds of opportunity to transform personal experiences into art. Social media permits creators to sidestep record labels, production studios, and other third parties and make their content available to millions of people around the world. This final action item focuses on the potential to create content we want to see, rather than simply challenging the content we do not.

While mental health in music is nothing new, musicians are increasingly being explicit about depression, anxiety, and other experiences in songs and conversations with audiences. The disclosures are applaudable (when proactive), and celebrities should continue recognizing the power of their platforms, whether they are athletes or actors, influencers or musicians. It is important mental health advocates lend additional support to these artists through social media comments and other means, because the overall media package communicates social norms about disclosing mental illness. Greater support might lead other respected athletes, actors, and musicians to openly discuss mental health, making the subject less taboo.

The power of stigma can be found in silence; through mass media, we have tools to break the silence, and in doing so, break stigma.

References

CineWell. (2022). Perks of Being a Wallflower. https://med.stanford.edu/psychiatry/special-initiatives/mediamh/cinewell/reviews.html#perks_of_being_awallflowerbyrachelb

Entertainment Industries Council. (2022). Vision. https://www.eiconline.org/about

Microsoft. (2022). Disability and neurodiversity community games and movies. https://www.xbox.com/en-us/promotions/disability-neurodiversity-community-picks

Mitropoulos, A. (2022). Blaming mass shootings on the nation's mental health crisis is 'harmful,' advocates say. ABC News. https://www.goodmorningamerica.com/news/story/blaming-mass-shootings-nations-mental-health-crisis-harmful-84973562

National Alliance on Mental Illness. (2022). NAMI statement on fatal shooting in Uvalde, Texas. NAMI. https://www.nami.org/Press-Media/Press-Releases/2022/NAMI-Statement-on-Fatal-Shooting-in-Uvalde-Texas

Parrott, S., Billings, A. C., Hakim, S. D., & Gentile, P. (2020). From# endthestigma to# realman: Stigma-challenging social media responses to NBA players' mental health disclosures. *Communication Reports, 33*(3), 148–160.

Roberts, K. (2018). 39 celebrities who have opened up about mental health. Harper's Bazaar. https://www.harpersbazaar.com/celebrity/latest/g15159447/celebrities-depression-anxiety-mental-health/

UNICEF (2020). How teenagers can protect their mental health during COVID-19. https://www.unicef.org/coronavirus/how-teenagers-can-protect-their-mental-health-during-coronavirus-covid-19

Index

Health Communication

Gary L. Kreps, Series Editor

This series examines the powerful influences of human and mediated communication in delivering care and promoting health.

Books analyze the ways that strategic communication humanizes and increases access to quality care as well as examining the use of communication to encourage proactive health promotion. The books describe strategies for addressing major health issues, such as reducing health disparities, minimizing health risks, responding to health crises, encouraging early detection and care, facilitating informed health decisionmaking, promoting coordination within and across health teams, overcoming health literacy challenges, designing responsive health information technologies, and delivering sensitive end-of-life care.

All books in the series are grounded in broad evidence-based scholarship and are vivid, compelling, and accessible to broad audiences of scholars, students, professionals, and laypersons.

For additional information about this series or for the submission of manuscripts, please contact:

Gary L. Kreps
University Distinguished Professor and Chair, Department of Communication
Director, Center for Health and Risk Communication
George Mason University Science & Technology 2, Suite 230, MS 3D6
Fairfax, VA 22030-4444
gkreps@gmu.edu